faithweaver™ youth bible studies

bible beginnings

www.faithweaver.com

Loveland, Colorado

Group

FaithWeaver Youth Bible Studies: Bible Beginnings

First Printing, 1999 Edition

Visit our web site: www.grouppublishing.com

Credits
Contributing Authors: Jay Ashscraft, Tim Baker, Erin McKay, Jane Vogel, and Michael Warden
Editor: Julie Meiklejohn
Creative Development Editors: Ivy Beckwith, Karl Leuthauser, Dave Thornton, and Paul Woods
Chief Creative Officer: Joani Schultz
Copy Editor: Bob Kretschman
Art Director: Jeff Spencer
Interior Graphic Designer: Matt Woods
Cover Art Director: Jim Misloski
Cover Designer: Cukjati Design
Computer Graphic Artist: Fred Schuth
Cover Photographer: Ted Gee Photography
Production Manager: Peggy Naylor

ISBN 0-7644-0911-5
Printed in the United States of America.

Contents

Why Do I Need FaithWeaver™ Youth Bible Studies?

A Search Institute study indicates that 86 percent of Christian teenagers do not read the Bible when they are by themselves. There are a variety of reasons, cited in *The Youth Bible*:

"I sometimes don't understand it, so I stop."—Mary in Nebraska

"I'm really confused."—Andrew in Michigan

"I don't know *how* to read the Bible."—Chris in Florida

Part of the reason teenagers find the Bible difficult to understand may be because their exposure to the "whole picture" of God's story has been somewhat limited. Young people often are exposed to the Bible in bits and pieces—a verse here, a passage there—and may never be given instruction about the Bible as a whole—where it came from, how the stories in the Bible fit together, and what the overall meaning of the Bible is. *FaithWeaver Youth Bible Studies* is designed specifically to help students see the "big picture"—starting with the very beginning of the story of God and his people. Through these studies, your youth will not only begin to see how all of the pieces fit together, they'll also see how the Bible's message is very relevant to their lives today.

Essential Components of FaithWeaver Youth Bible Studies

Many elements within *FaithWeaver Youth Bible Studies* bring exciting benefits to your youth. Here are the highlights:

• **Each study is centered around a Key Question that can be answered through the Bible passage and applied to teenagers' lives.** The Key Question each week leads youth to examine Scripture and discover the answer. Teenagers then examine that answer to determine what relevance it has to them. Before the study is over, teenagers also will be challenged to take steps toward active application of that Bible principle, weaving their faith into their lives.

• **Each study teaches to multiple intelligences.** Multiple intelligences describe the different ways in which students are smart. For example, some students may have a great deal of kinesthetic intelligence and learn best using hands-on activities. Other students may have more verbal intelligence; these students learn best by processing things through writing or discussing. Because some of your teenagers may be smart in ways that are different from the ways in which you are smart, resist the impulse to skip activities that don't naturally attract you; they may be just what will resonate with some of your students.

• **Each study provides adaptation tips for younger or older students.** These tips—containing various age-appropriate options for many of the activities—help you customize each study for the needs of your teenagers.

• **Each study contains an activity to help students explore the historical and cultural context of each Bible story.** The Historical Context box and activity provide valuable Scriptural context information as well as a meaningful way to help students dig a little deeper into the Bible passage.

• **This book comes with a compact disc of great new Christian songs and Music Connection pages.** Each study utilizes these resources to connect with your teenagers through a medium they love—music!

• **Each study includes a "Taking It Home" page.** This page, which you can mail home or distribute during your meeting, provides fun, in-depth activities and discussions to help teenagers explore what they've learned with their families.

• **Each study provides a "Faith Journal" option with a solid assessment question that will help you discover how well your students are learning as well as help you develop better relationships with them.** At the end of each study, you'll be prompted to have students respond to a "sum-up" question on index cards. You'll collect the cards and take some time during the next week to write affirming responses and comments to what they've written. For example, you may write things such as "I'm glad you gained such a knowledge of God's love during this study" or "Hang in there; God is walking beside you. I'm praying for you." Make these comments as personal and meaningful as you can; it will mean a great deal to your students. At the beginning of the next study, you'll be prompted to return the index cards with your comments on them to your students. It's also a good idea to keep copies of the cards in a notebook or a box so that you'll have an ongoing record of how your students are doing.

Some other options for the "Faith Journal" cards might be to have students write any prayer concerns they may have or to have them write their own questions about the topic.

If you notice a student response that seems troubling, be sure to touch base with the student sometime right before or after your next meeting. If a student seems to be having problems you're not comfortable handling, ask your pastor or your Christian education director for help.

These innovative, effective learning techniques will transform your classroom into a relational, fun, and caring place for learning. *FaithWeaver Youth Bible Studies* will help you change the lives of your teenagers and ensure that authentic learning takes place.

About Your Students

FaithWeaver Youth Bible Studies was written and developed by people who have significant experience working with teenagers. We've designed the studies to be interesting, beneficial, and age-appropriate for your youth. As you use the studies to encourage their faith and growth, you might want to keep the following in mind:

• Teenagers' spirituality is, above all, **personal.** They are ready to embrace a more personal relationship with Christ.

• Teenagers' spirituality is **relational.** Relationships with family, friends, peers, and teachers are of high importance to teenagers; they can be encouraged and challenged to examine those relationships in the light of a personal relationship with Christ.

• Teenagers' spirituality is beginning to focus on **future living.** As teenagers look toward their futures, they can be encouraged to consider how their current choices can create their responses to Christ's call in the future.

• Teenagers' spirituality is **multi-faceted.** Teenagers hope to discover how their faith can touch and be reflected in all aspects of their lives.

• Teenagers' spirituality is affected by their **physical and mental development.** As their brains develop and their bodies change, teenagers' capacity to think undergoes a dramatic shift, and their worlds broaden. They become more capable of thinking cognitively and metaphorically.

There's More...

FaithWeaver Youth Bible Studies is just one of the components of Group's FaithWeaver™ family of Christian growth resources. This system of resources is composed of three major elements and other supporting materials. The major elements are FaithWeaver Bible Curriculum, FaithWeaver Children's Church, and FaithWeaver Midweek (to be released in 2000). Supporting materials include Home Link resources for families and Pastor Link resources for pastors. Any one of the elements can be used without the others. However, using all of them together will help your church's families learn and grow in faith both at church and at home in a way no single book can.

• **FaithWeaver Bible Curriculum**—Designed for use in Sunday school, this portion of the system concentrates on education. Infants through adults cover the same Bible story, learning about it and applying it at appropriate levels for all age groupings. When you use *FaithWeaver Youth Bible Studies*, you can tie teenagers into a bigger picture of all-church learning.

• **FaithWeaver Children's Church**—This program includes both preschool and elementary children, with options for joint and separate activities for each. The focus of this element is to learn about worship and to practice it together, while connecting with the story or topic covered in FaithWeaver Bible Curriculum. Here's an opportunity for teenagers to help lead and support children.

• **FaithWeaver Midweek**—Still in development, this program focuses on relationships and service, giving children opportunities to demonstrate their faith in their lives. This will be another leadership opportunity for teenagers to mentor younger children.

• **FaithWeaver Home Link**—Two significant resources to help weave faith into life at home are the Adult FaithWeaver Bible Curriculum and the "Driving Home the Point" weekly page. Within the adult curriculum, a segment written especially for parents and caregivers provides them ways to continue the faith development of their children at home. And the Driving Home the Point weekly pages contain devotions, discussions, extra activities, and suggestions to keep the family growing in faith together after leaving the church building.

• **FaithWeaver Pastor Link**—This element also contains two resources. The first is the Pastor Handbook 1999-2000, which helps the pastor know what's going on in the education program. Using it, the pastor can choose to connect messages or church services with what's being taught. The second resource is a yearly book of children's sermons, *FaithWeaver Children's Messages*, that allows the pastor to present a children's sermon each week that supplements what children are studying in Sunday school.

• **FaithWeaver Internet Link**— Please visit our Web site at www.faithweaver.com to download FaithWeaver materials or to obtain more information about the system.

Creation 101

Genesis 1:1–2:3

1

God Creates the World

key question: How did the world come to be?

study focus: Teenagers will explore the "how" behind Creation as they discover what God reveals about himself through his creation.

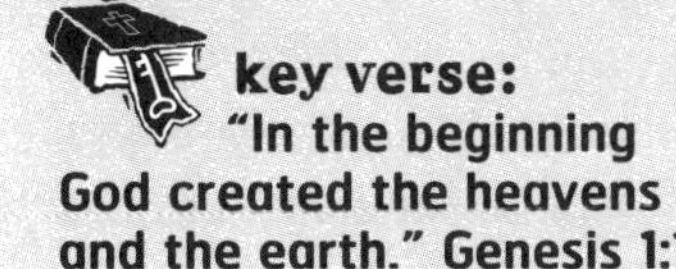

key verse: "In the beginning God created the heavens and the earth." Genesis 1:1

A Look at the Study

Study Sequence	Minutes	What Students Will Do	Classroom Supplies
Getting Started	5 to 10	**In the Beginning**— Examine the story of Creation.	
Bible Story Exploration	5 to 10	**God's Great Act of Creation**—Explore background information about the Creation story.	"Historical Context" copies (p. 11)
	25 to 30	**Creation Observation**—Explore specific areas of creation as they discuss characteristics of God.	"Observation Log" handouts (p. 15), pens, newsprint, marker
Bible Application	5 to 10	**God Is So Good**—Compose a litany about God's qualities and thank God for his wonderful creation.	Bibles
	up to 5	**Faith Journal**—Explore the Key Question and respond in writing.	Index cards, pens
Music Connection	5 to 10	**Awesome God**—Describe the Creator God. Use this option at an appropriate time in the study.	Bibles, CD: "Awesome God" (Track 1), CD player

Age-Level Insight

As they go through the study, teenagers will be concerned with *how* God made everything. School science classes may seem to contradict church teaching about Creation. Treat students' questions with respect, show them what respected Christian scholars say about the subject, and continue to emphasize that God made everything. We may not know exactly *how* God did it, but we know that he did it. Use the majesty of Creation as a way of calling teenagers' attention to the wonders of God's character.

Getting Started

In the Beginning

Have students form three groups (a group can be made up of one or more people), and assign each group one of these phrases: "And God said...," "and it was so," and "and God saw that it was good."

SAY **I'm going to read the story of Creation to you. I'll pause during my reading when one of these phrases comes up. When I point to your group, you'll need to say your assigned phrase with enthusiasm! I'd also like you to be thinking about what it might have been like to witness God's creation of our world.**

Read **Genesis 1:1–2:3** aloud. Use inflection and gestures to awaken students to the drama of this familiar passage.

When you've finished reading,

SAY **Now in your group, I'd like you to compare thoughts about what it might have been like to witness Creation. Think of three adjectives that describe what you thought.**

Have groups share their adjectives, and then

ASK **• What do you think God revealed about himself through his act of Creation?**

• What does this story tell us about how the world came to be?

SAY **Even before the words in the Bible were written down, God was revealing things about his identity through Creation! Today we're going to take some time to explore the things God tells us about himself and the great act of Creation through the amazing world God created.**

Bible Story Exploration

God's Great Act of Creation

Give each group a copy of the "Historical Context" box (p. 11).

SAY **I'd like you to begin your exploration of the Creation story by learning and teaching each other some historical background information. I'm going to assign each group two paragraphs from the "Historical Context" box. In your group, you'll need to read through the information and then decide together on a creative, quick way to present the**

Teacher Skillbuilder

Throughout this book, the studies will guide you to teach to "multiple intelligences." Multiple intelligences describe the different ways in which students are smart. For example, some students may have a great deal of kinesthetic intelligence and learn best using hands-on activities. Other students may have more verbal intelligence; these students learn best by processing things through writing or discussing. Because some of your teenagers may be smart in ways that are different from the ways in which you are smart, resist the impulse to skip activities that don't naturally attract you; they may be just what will resonate with some of your students. For example, teenagers who love to classify, categorize, and list their observations will relish the investigative portion of this study, while visually oriented students will prize the opportunity to sketch their observations. More verbal students will be swept up in the dramatic reading that opens this study.

information you've learned to the rest of the class. For example, you might want to create a short skit, compose a litany, or do a dramatic reading. Make sure that everyone in your group is involved in the presentation.

Assign one group the first two paragraphs, one group the second two paragraphs, and one group the third two paragraphs. Give groups a few minutes to read through their information and create their presentations. Then have groups share their presentations with the whole class, one at a time. After they're finished,

ASK
- **What was one interesting fact you learned from another group's presentation?**
- **What does the information you just learned about tell you about God?**
- **What does the information tell you about why the world was created?**

SAY **Now let's learn more about our creator, God.**

To add drama to your reading, play dramatic music in the background—any piece of music that builds in intensity would be terrific. Richard Strauss' "Thus Spake Zarathustra" (better known as the theme song from the movie *2001: A Space Odyssey*) is an excellent example.

Historical Context | Genesis 1:1–2:3

The book of Genesis gives us the beginnings. Note that this is not the beginning of God; God has existed eternally. Neither is it just the beginning of our world. It is, rather, the beginnings of God's working with humans. That's the meaning of the Greek word from which the name "Genesis" came. What better place to start a new Sunday school year than at the beginning of God's story!

Elohim is the Hebrew name used for God in Genesis 1:1. It's interesting that the name is plural, but the verb "created" is singular. Even though God existed in three persons, the action of creating the universe was a unified action. One God, three persons, one plan.

Genesis 1:1–2:3 describes a vast variety of things God created, but the focus is not so much on the creation as it is on the Creator. Nine times in this passage we read, "God said" and then some variation of "It was so." God spoke our universe, our planet, and humankind into existence. And what God did was good.

The word translated "good" here is a common Hebrew word that means "just as it should be." God looked at what he had done and knew that it was right. He didn't mess up. God knew what he was doing.

What God was doing was creating a bountiful, beautiful home for the treasured beings that he would create last. Notice that God created many of each thing: not just one tree, but "seed-bearing plants and trees...according to their various kinds"; not just one star, but "lights in the expanse of the sky"; not just one fish, but "every living and moving thing with which the water teems"; not just one horse, but "all the creatures that move along the ground." God prepared a marvelous earth for his crowning creation to enjoy.

And then God created humans. We are a vital part of everything good that God made.

When God finished creating the heavens and the earth "in all their vast array," he rested. Why? God wasn't tired. God didn't need to rest. No, God rested as a signal that Creation was complete. It became a holy day—a day to reflect on the wonder of what God had done, a day to smile and to know that it was good.

Creation Observation

Give each teenager an "Observation Log" handout (p. 15) and a pen. Let each student choose the area of investigation that most interests him or her and form an investigation group with no more than three other people.

SAY **As we learn how the world came to be, we can also learn a lot about the God who brought the world into being. For instance, when we observe symmetry in leaves and flowers, we learn that the God who created them is a God of order, not of randomness and chaos.**

Tell groups they each have about fifteen minutes to find two or more samples of their chosen subject (for example, a group might find leaves from two different kinds of plants, two bugs, or two people) and study the samples. Have members of each group note their observations in their observation logs. If possible, send students outside for this part of the study. Encourage students to be creative if they have trouble finding samples. For example, a group studying people could go to the church nursery or simply study its own members.

After about fifteen minutes, bring the investigation groups together, and have each share its findings with the rest of the class. After each presentation,

ASK • **What new or unusual things did you notice as you made such close observations?**

• **What do your observations show you about how the world came to be?**

ASK • **God said that what he made was good. What are some good characteristics of the creation you observed?**

As students share what they've learned about God, have a volunteer write their observations on a sheet of newsprint.

Bible Application

God Is So Good

Point to the list of things the class learned about God, and ask teenagers each to think of one or two of God's qualities that are particularly meaningful to him or her. Distribute Bibles, and have students form a circle. Ask a volunteer to read the Key Verse aloud.

SAY **We're going to create a litany to parallel the dramatic reading that started our study. We'll go around the circle, and each person will say the Key Verse aloud—with a difference. When it's your turn, include the qualities of God that you find meaningful as you say the verse. For example, you might say, "In the beginning God, who gives his creatures everything they need to survive, created the heavens and the earth."**

Tip From the Trenches

Limit each investigation group to no more than four people so that every member stays involved. It's OK if more than four people want to investigate the same topic; simply have those students form two or more groups.

for Younger teenagers

Challenge younger teenagers to come up with a creative way of recording what they've learned about our creative God. Instead of simply writing observations on newsprint, for example, students could include the ideas from the different groups in a work of art, a song, or a video.

Tip From the Trenches

To help strengthen the connection between church and home, photocopy the "Taking It Home" page at the end of this study, and either distribute copies to students before they leave or mail them home. Encourage students to complete the reading, activities, and discussion with their families during the coming week.

Go around the circle, letting each student personalize the Key Verse.

Conclude your study with an "open eyes" prayer. Go outside and form a circle with everyone facing the outside of the circle. Then go around the circle, letting each person praise God for something in creation that the person can see from where he or she is standing.

Faith Journal

Give students each an index card and a pen. Have teenagers write their names and answers to the following question on their index cards:

- What do your observations about creation tell you about God's identity and character? Explain.

Have teenagers return their index cards to you. Before you meet with the group again, take some time to write personal responses to your students on their index cards. You may want to keep a notebook or a box containing copies of these index cards.

For more information about the Faith Journal option, refer to page 5 in the Introduction.

for OLDER teenagers

Older teenagers may be struggling with the creation vs. evolution debate. Use the quotes and discussion questions in the "Creation vs. Evolution" box (p. 13) to help teenagers grapple with this topic and to add another level to this study.

Creation vs. Evolution

Read these quotes, and then discuss the questions that follow in your group.

- "A natural and fundamental question to ask, on learning of these incredibly intricately interlocking pieces of software and hardware is: 'How did they ever get started in the first place?' It is truly a baffling thing...there are various theories on the origin of life. They all run aground on this most central of all central questions: 'How did the Genetic Code, along with the mechanisms for its translation..., originate?" (Douglas Hofstadter, quoted by Philip Yancey in Christianity Today magazine)
- "The laws of probability point to the existence of a Creator. For example, for even the simplest amino acid to have formed by chance, the earth would have to be at least twelve times older than scientists say it is. The fact that amino acids—which are the building blocks of life—exist at all indicates an intelligent Creator." (Michael D. Warden, *Why Creation Matters)*
- What do these quotes tell you about the debate between creation and evolution?
- Do you think we can trust the Bible to be accurate about such scientific things as the beginning of life? Explain.
- How does one's belief regarding creation and evolution affect one's faith?

[mu/Sic] Music Connection

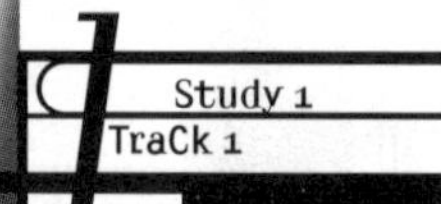

idea:listen

[m u s i c]

Have teenagers create a list of adjectives and descriptions of the Creator God, such as "powerful" or "mighty."

track 1:
Then play the song "Awesome God" from the CD. As students listen, have them write down other descriptions of God that are included in the song. When the song is finished, have students share their descriptions.

ASK • **How does creation show that God is awesome?**

Then read **Psalm 19:1-6** aloud.

ASK • **This song and the psalm serve as reminders of how awesome God is. What are some other things you could do to remind yourself or others of the awesomeness of God?**

Awesome God

(recorded by Reggae Worship)

Chorus:
Our God is an awesome God;
He reigns from heaven above
With wisdom, power, and love,
Our God is an awesome God!

When he rolls up his sleeves,
He ain't just "puttin' on the ritz."
(Our God is an awesome God.)
There is thunder in his footsteps
And lightning in his fists.
(Our God is an awesome God.)
The Lord wasn't joking
When he kicked 'em out of Eden;
It wasn't for no reason
That he shed his blood.
His return is very close,
And so you better be believing that
Our God is an awesome God.

Chorus

And when the sky was starless
In the void of the night,
(Our God is an awesome God.)
He spoke into the darkness
And created the light.
(Our God is an awesome God.)
Judgment and wrath
He poured out on Sodom;
Mercy and grace he gave us at the cross.
I hope that we have not
Too quickly forgotten that
Our God is an awesome God.

our creator is awesome

Observation Log

idea:observe

Choose one of the following areas of investigation, and then form a group with one to three other people who are interested in investigating the same subject:

- plants
- animals
- human beings.

Find at least two samples from your area of investigation, observe them closely, and record your observations here. Look for all details of your samples, including color, shape, size, and any unusual markings. List any other interesting things you notice about your samples, including sounds they make and the way they move.

- Describe your samples, using either words or sketches.

- Compare the samples by listing their similarities and differences.

Similarities	Differences

- What conclusions, if any, can you draw about the relationship between your samples?

- What can you determine about how your samples function or survive? (How are they equipped to get what they need to survive?)

- What questions do your observations raise about your samples?

- What do your observations show you about God? about how the world came to be?

[think]

research required

idea:discuss Talking About It

take home | everywhere

Driving Home the Point:

"To think you can find God only in a church is as absurd as thinking you can find great works of art only in a gallery. To suppose God is confined beneath a steeple is to suppose drama is confined to the stage, music to the concert hall, or animals to the zoo. Look about! God, as with all of these other things, can be witnessed right outside your bedroom window. You can catch a glimpse of heaven in the petals of a flower, the smile of a child, the light of the sun, the reflection of a puddle, the embrace of a lover. All of these things should drive you to worship the Lord, because God can be clearly seen and understood from what he has made...

"Some people will one day stand before God and try to excuse their lack of belief by saying, 'I never knew you because I never went to church.'

" 'Nonsense!' God will probably reply. 'Did you never take a walk, look into the star-spangled sky, or watch a tree catch fire at sunset? I surrounded you twenty-four hours a day with evidence of my love and glory. You were just too busy to notice.'" **(S. Rickly Christian,** *Alive***)**

Talking At Home:

Read **Romans 1:20** and discuss the following questions as a family:

- **According to this verse, what does God's creation tell us about his nature?**

- **What does God's incredible attention to detail tell us about the way he feels about his creation?**

What parts of the natural world do you especially enjoy? You may think of favorite vacation spots or physical examples, such as a family pet. Discuss how you feel about God when you're enjoying your favorite parts of nature.

Handmade

Genesis 2:4-22

2

God Creates Adam and Eve

key question: How do we know we're important to God?

study focus: Teenagers will see themselves as God's special, handmade creations.

key verse: "I praise you because I am fearfully and wonderfully made; your works are wonderful, I know that full well." Psalm 139:14

A Look at the Study

Study Sequence	Minutes	What Students Will Do	Classroom Supplies
Getting Started	10 to 15	**The Meaning of Life**—Explore several different people's views of the meaning and value of human life.	
Bible Story Exploration	5 to 10	**The Creation of Humans**—Explore background information about the creation of humans.	Bibles, "Historical Context" copies (p. 20), paper, pens
	20 to 25	**In His Image**—Experience the story of the creation of humans as they determine their responsibilities as modern humans.	Bibles, modeling clay, various symbols of human experiences and responsibilities, index cards, pens, "Handmade" handouts (p. 24)
Bible Application	5 to 10	**Unique and Special**—Create symbols to represent what life means to them.	Bibles, paper, markers
	up to 5	**Faith Journal**—Explore the Key Question and respond in writing.	Index cards, pens
Music Connection	5 to 10	**You Are Loved**—Discuss humans' importance to God. Use this option at an appropriate time in the study.	"You Are Loved" lyric copies (p. 23), pens, CD: "You Are Loved" (Track 2), CD player

Age-Level Insight

Adolescence is a time of great physical, emotional, and social change. Almost overnight, youth find their bodies changing and discover new emotions. They feel the pressure to discover themselves, the desire to differentiate themselves from their parents, and the need to choose a life path. Young people need to be consistently reminded that God created them the way they are for specific purposes. It's a good time to remind teenagers of God's good and unique creation of each of them. He created each teenager with gifts and talents, and each one has something to offer the world.

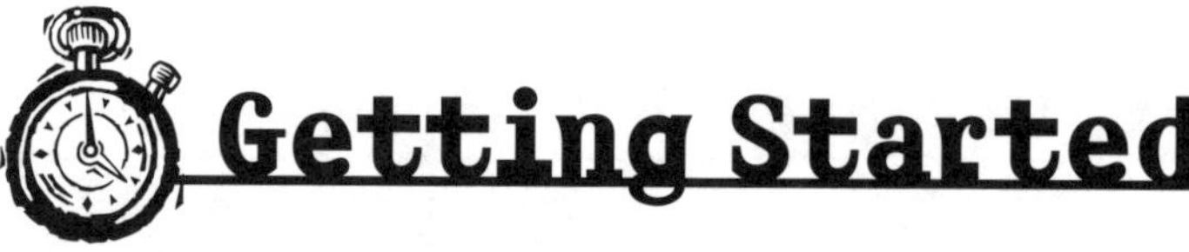

The Meaning of Life

Have teenagers form groups of four, and assign each group one of the following identities: the Unabomber (who admitted to killing people by placing bombs in packages to be mailed), Adolf Hitler (who caused millions of Jews to be killed during World War II), Jack Kevorkian (who provides assisted suicide for people with terminal illnesses), Saddam Hussein (the leader of Iraq who brought about the Persian Gulf War), Mother Teresa (who led a missionary group in India), and Jonas Salk (who developed the first vaccine against polio).

SAY **In your group, I'd like you to spend a few minutes coming up with a brief statement that you think expresses your assigned character's view of human life. For example, Adolf Hitler's statement might be, "Only German people are of any value. All other human life can be disposed of or experimented on."**

Give groups a minute to work, and then have a volunteer from each group report his or her group's statement.

ASK
- **How do you think your assigned person's view of the value of human life influences what that person does** (or did)**?**
- **How do you think your view of the value of human life may influence your actions and decisions? Give some examples.**

Then bring the issue closer to home by reading aloud and discussing the following news story.

A True Story

Scott Krueger had everything going for him. He was a top student, a fine athlete, good-looking, and well-liked. He had been accepted to MIT. As he started his freshman year, a bright future seemed to stretch ahead of him.

That future ended only a few weeks into Scott's first semester. His frat house specified an amount that Scott and the other members of his class had to drink to be part of the fraternity. Trying to drink his share, Scott passed out, choked on his own vomit, and, after fifty-seven hours on a ventilator, died.

Reactions to Scott's death varied. When Scott's mother called the frat house to try to understand how the tragedy could have happened, one member told her, "You have to understand—this was a *very* big night at our fraternity house." Scott's pastor, in his funeral message, said, "We are grieving for a brilliant, beautiful, Christ-centered man who was killed by a system...a system that...builds manhood and brotherhood through alcohol consumption and parties."

(John McCormick and Claudia Kalb, "Dying for a Drink," Newsweek, June 15, 1998)

Last Week's Impact

As teenagers arrive, greet them warmly and ask follow-up questions to review last week's study and Key Verse. Ask questions such as "What were some of your family members' favorite parts of nature?" and "What does God's creation tell us about who he is?"

If you used the Faith Journal option last week, take this time to return your students' index cards to them.

for Younger teenagers

If you think younger teenagers may not recognize the assigned names, briefly explain who each is or substitute generic categories such as terrorists, biochemical warfare scientists, doctors who provide "assisted suicide," or people in favor of "ethnic cleansing." Be sure to include a few positive categories as well, such as people who do research to cure diseases.

Have kids form pairs and discuss these questions:

- **What do you think of the fraternity member's response to Scott's mother? Explain.**
- **How would you summarize the fraternity member's view of human life? Scott's pastor's view? Which view do you most agree with?**

- **Do you think that Scott's life is important to God? Why or why not?**

for Younger teenagers

Get younger teenagers started by having them formulate their own ideas about the meaning and value of human life. Encourage them to compare their ideas to the possible definitions of the people listed.

Bible Story Exploration

The Creation of Humans

Students should remain in pairs. Give each student a copy of the "Historical Context" box (p. 20), a Bible, paper, and a pen.

SAY **I'd like you to begin your study of God's creation of humans by studying some background information. I'll give each pair a topic to research. As you read the information I've given you, I'd like you to be thinking about the topic I've assigned you. When you're finished reading, I'd like you to write a brief news article that tells about your assigned topic.**

Assign pairs the following topics (it's OK if more than one pair has the same topic):

- Differences and similarities in the Creation accounts;
- How and why Adam was created;
- How and why Eve was created.

Invite students to take their research further by including information from the Bible story.

Give pairs a few minutes to read the information and write their news articles, and then have them present the articles to the whole class.

ASK • **What does this information tell you about God?**

- **Do you think humans are important to God? Why or why not?**

SAY **Let's learn more about God's creation of humans.**

Historical Context | Genesis 2:4-22

As we look at this passage, it's good to note that God did not give us in the Bible a precise chronological history of our world. God communicates to us through the Bible to give us a spiritual message—to tell us of his love and his plan for us. Because of this, we can't always expect everything we read in the Bible to fall in strict chronological order.

Some scholars see problems in the differences between the accounts of the creation of humans in Genesis 1 and Genesis 2. Others, however, see the account in chapter 2 as an elaboration of chapter 1. But notice the emphasis in both accounts: God did it. The emphasis in this story is not upon the creature, but upon the Creator. The use of two names of God, "Lord God," is a Hebrew way of showing emphasis. The point is the greatness of the God who created us.

In Genesis 2:7 we see a bit of the "how" of Adam's creation. It's interesting to note that humans were the first of creation not simply spoken into being. This account tells us of God's personally forming Adam out of the earth. And then one more difference appears: God breathed life into Adam, and he became a living being. Many here translate "being" as "soul." And no other creature was given that designation. Genesis 1:27 tells us that humans were created in God's image. And after the creation of humans, God announced that his creation was not only "good," it was "very good" (Genesis 1:31). We definitely are God's *very* special creation.

Adam's need for a mate, someone to stand alongside him, didn't come as a surprise to God. The parade of animals for Adam to name had a purpose beyond the naming: It pointed out to Adam that he was alone, that he didn't have a mate like him—someone who could share his life. Someone who, with him, could carry on the procreation of humankind. After helping Adam come to this realization, God created woman.

Many appropriate conclusions have been drawn from Eve's being created from Adam's rib—from his side—such as the intent that they work side by side, that they be equal to each other in standing before God, and that they become "one flesh" in the bond of marriage. However, Adam lost a rib to make Eve. Without her, he was incomplete. And without Adam, Eve wouldn't have existed. Both had strengths—and weaknesses. But together, man and woman became a whole being, able to stand together and support each other against the forces that oppose them—just as God had planned from the start.

In His Image

Designate three areas of the room as different learning stations. At station 1, set out lumps of modeling clay. At station 2, set out various symbols of human experiences and responsibilities, such as a magnifying glass, a picture of a family, and a branch from a tree. At station 3, set out index cards.

Have students work with their partners from the previous activity. Give each pair a Bible, a pen, and a copy of the "Handmade" handout (p. 24).

SAY **With your partner, follow the directions on your handout and discuss the questions. Spend about five minutes at your first station and then move to the next station. It doesn't matter what order you visit the stations as long as you complete all three stations in the next fifteen minutes.**

As pairs move to the stations, direct them so that about one-third of the pairs goes to each station. To keep students moving at an appropriate pace, give them a signal every five minutes.

After about fifteen minutes, bring everyone together. Invite volunteers to share their responses to the first station.

ASK • **How does the Bible's view of human life compare or contrast with some of the views we talked about earlier?**

• **If Scott or his frat brothers had been thinking of people as God's handmade creations, how might that have influenced their actions and attitudes?**

Invite volunteers to share their job descriptions from station 2.

ASK • **How does it make you feel to know that God has given *you* so much authority and responsibility in his world?**

• **When do you most see yourself as God's image-bearer with an important job to do?**

Collect the cards from station 3 and read as many of them aloud as time allows. After each,

ASK questions such as:

• **When are you likely to have to face this kind of decision?**

• **How might the choice that leads to death be displeasing to God?**

• **How could seeing yourself as God's handmade creation influence the decision you make?**

Bible Application

Unique and Special

Have students turn to **Psalm 139:14** and follow along as a volunteer reads the verse aloud.

ASK

• **What difference does it make that God made you—you personally—as a special, handmade creation?**

SAY **I'd like you to think back on the statements about human life that you came up with during the first activity.**

Hand out paper and markers.

Teacher Skillbuilder

When teenagers work in small groups, they may need guidance to get the most out of the experience. Circulate among your students as they work, listening to make sure they're staying on task and answering any questions they have. If a student starts to goof off or become distracted, a hand on his or her shoulder and a quiet "Let's not lose our focus" usually will get the student back on track.

For Extra Impact

Provide business-card-sized magnets with adhesive on the front (available from office supply and hobby stores), and have students write or draw their statements or symbols on paper cut to fit the magnets. Encourage students to post their magnets in their school lockers to remind them that they are God's handmade creations.

Tip From the Trenches

To help strengthen the connection between church and home, photocopy the "Taking It Home" page at the end of this study, and either distribute copies to students before they leave or mail them home. Encourage students to complete the reading, activities, and discussion with their families during the coming week.

SAY **Now I'd like you to write or draw a personal statement or symbol illustrating what you believe about human life. Use Psalm 139:14 to help you.**

Close with a prayer of praise to God for creating each person special.

Faith Journal

Give students each an index card and a pen. Have teenagers write their names and answers to this question on their index cards:

- How can knowing your amazing importance to God affect your actions and decisions?

Have teenagers return their index cards to you. Before you meet with the group again, take some time to write personal responses to your students on their index cards. You may want to keep a notebook or a box containing copies of these index cards.

For more information about the Faith Journal option, refer to page 5 in the Introduction.

Music Connection

[mu/Sic]

idea:listen

Give each student a copy of the lyrics for "You Are Loved" and a pen. Tell students that you'll be playing the song; while they listen, they'll need to underline each place where the singer seems to feel that he isn't important to God.

track 2: Play "You Are Loved." When the song is finished, have students share what they underlined.

ASK
- **How does God's detailed and painstaking creation of humans show how important we are to God?**
- **Why do you think people sometimes believe they aren't important to God?**
- **How can we remind ourselves or other people of humans' importance to God?**

Have students form pairs and choose one of the underlined passages. In pairs, have students use what they learned in today's lesson about humans' importance to God to write a response to someone who may be feeling the emotions expressed in their chosen passage.

You Are Loved (Remix)

(recorded by Altar Boys)

Hard times in the city,
They just don't go away.
Out here, the anger and frustration
Never takes a holiday (yeah).
I've seen the faces,
And how can I turn away?
Baby, I'm talkin' to you;
Yeah, I'm tryin' to get through-
God cares about you more than you think (yeah).

Chorus:
To all the hearts that have been broken:
To all the dreamers with abandoned dreams:
To everybody in need of a friend now:
You are loved! You are loved!
To all the rebels wounded in battle:
To all the rockers that have lost that beat:
To all the users all used up now:
You are loved! You are loved!

In a flash, he walked out-
He just couldn't take any more.
What he thought was happiness
Just turned around and smashed on the floor (yeah).

I see his face,
And how can I turn away?
Hey man, I'm talkin' to you;
Yeah, I'm tryin' to get through-
God cares about you more than you think.
Listen...

Chorus

You don't need to stand alone;
There's someone you can hold on to.
I want to let you know-
You are loved! You are loved!

This world is such a hard place;
You just get lost in the crowd.
To some you're just a number;
To others you're just somebody hangin' around now.
I see the faces,
And I'm not gonna turn away.
Yeah, I'm talkin' to you;
I'm tryin' to get through-
God cares about you more than you think.
So listen...

Chorus (repeat twice)

[music]

god loves us

Handmade

idea:created

[t h i n k]

beginning

With a partner, spend about five minutes at each station. You can complete the stations in any order.

Station 1:

1. Read **Genesis 2:4-7, 21-22.**
2. Take some of the modeling clay and shape it into something. With your partner, discuss this question:
    - What does the physical molding of the clay suggest to you about God's relationship to human beings?
3. Read **Psalm 139:14**. Share with your partner one wonderful thing about you that God has made.

Station 2:

1. Read **Genesis 2:8-15, 19-20a.**
2. Work with your partner to create a job description for Adam based on these verses. (Hint: Look also at **Genesis 1:28-29.**)

Position: First human
Job title: God's image-bearer
Responsibilities: ______________________________

____

____

____

3. What does the job description look like for us today? Look at the items at the station to get some ideas (for example, think about ways to use the magnifying glass to learn from and take care of God's world). Then work with your partner to write a job description that defines how you think God wants you to relate to the rest of his creation.

Position: Modern-day human
Job title: God's image-bearer
Responsibilities: ______________________________

____

____

____

Station 3:

1. Read **Genesis 2:16-17**.
2. With your partner, think of some life-or-death choices that you or your peers face. Make these realistic, everyday kinds of choices. On one side of an index card, write the choice that could result in death; on the other side, write an alternative action to take. One example of a choice might be "Getting in a car with someone who's drunk;" an alternative action might be "Deciding to walk or call my parents." Try to write several cards in the time you have at this station.

Driving Home the Point:

"You aren't an accident. You weren't mass-produced. You aren't an assembly-line product. You were deliberately planned, specifically gifted, and lovingly positioned on this earth by the Master Craftsman."

(Max Lucado)

Talking At Home:

Read **Genesis 1:27** as a family and discuss the following questions:

- What do you think it means to be created in God's image?

- What does this verse tell you about your importance to God?

How did each member of the family join the family? Was it by marriage, through birth, through adoption, or through blending? What makes each family member special? (Yes, even your little brother!)

He's no assembly-line God

Exit From Eden

Genesis 3:1-24

3

Adam and Eve Sin

key question: Why do we sin?

study focus: Teenagers will recognize that Adam and Eve's sin created a separation between humans and God that only Jesus Christ can bridge.

key verse: "...for all have sinned and fall short of the glory of God." Romans 3:23

A Look at the Study

Study Sequence	Minutes	What Students Will Do	Classroom Supplies
Getting Started	5 to 10	**Conflict Creations**—Create skits to demonstrate separation caused by conflicts with other people.	
Bible Story Exploration	5 to 10	**Sin's Great Temptation**—Explore background information about Adam and Eve's sin.	"Historical Context" copies (p. 29), pens, paper
	15 to 20	**Contaminated by Sin**—Experience the Bible story and then identify and illustrate the conflict, the consequences, and the solution.	Bibles, "Exit From Eden" handouts (p. 34), pens, poster board, markers, old magazines, scissors, glue
	5 to 10	**Purified by Christ**—Experience an object study that demonstrates how, even though our lives are hopelessly contaminated by sin, God offers purity through Christ.	Bibles, two clear glasses, water, a bowl, food coloring
Bible Application	5 to 10	**Bridging the Gap**—Reflect silently about their own conflicts and separation from God.	Bible
	up to 5	**Faith Journal**—Explore the Key Question and respond in writing.	Index cards, pens
Music Connection	5 to 10	**I Need You**—Explore times they need God's forgiveness. Use this option at an appropriate time in the study.	Paper, black markers, CD: "I Need You" (Track 3), CD player

Age-Level Insight

During adolescence, teenagers begin to internalize the morals and values they have been taught. Adolescents can look at the larger issues of right and wrong and apply those discoveries to their own personal struggles with morality. When discussing right and wrong with teenagers, continue to help them discover what God says about particular issues while helping them examine why God may have said what he did. Also, help teenagers discover the role God's forgiveness plays as they struggle to live within God's moral parameters.

Last Week's Impact

As teenagers arrive, greet them warmly and ask follow-up questions to review last week's study and Key Verse. Ask questions such as "What were some of the God-given qualities you saw in your siblings or parents?" and "How do you know that you're important to God?"

If you used the Faith Journal option last week, take this time to return your students' index cards to them.

for OLDER teenagers

You may want to give older teenagers different options for this part of the study. For example, they may want to spend a few minutes journalizing about a personal situation that fits one of these categories, or they might like to do a pair-share discussion about different types of conflict (and subsequent separation) they've experienced personally. Follow with the debriefing questions at the end of the activity.

Getting Started

Conflict Creations

Form groups of three to five people. Assign each group one of the following casts of characters:

- A teenager and parents fighting over the teenager's curfew;
- A teenager angry at friends for leaving him or her out of their plans;
- A boyfriend jealous of his girlfriend's friendships with other guys;
- A student and a teacher arguing about the fairness of a test grade.

Give the groups about five minutes to plan skits using the following guidelines:

- The skit must show a conflict that causes a separation between two of the characters. (The separation can be temporary.)
- The skit should not resolve the conflict.
- Every member of the group must be involved as characters in conflict, as additional characters (such as friends of the characters in conflict), or as props (such as tables, cars, or lockers).

After about five minutes, have each group present its skit.

ASK • **Which of these characters or conflicts do you identify with most? Explain.**

? • **Why are there conflicts in so many of our relationships?**

• **In your experience, what usually happens to a relationship when conflict enters it?**

Bible Story Exploration

Sin's Great Temptation

SAY **Now we're going to look at another drama—the drama of the very first conflict and separation.**

Have students stay in their groups from the previous activity. Give each student a copy of the "Historical Context" box (p. 29), a pen, and a blank piece of paper.

SAY **I'd like you to begin your examination of sin's separation by studying some background information. I'll assign each group one of two themes: "sin" or "God's love." As you read the information I've given you in your groups, I'd like you to think about the theme I've assigned to your group. When**

you're finished, jot notes about any information you've discovered about your theme in the reading. Then, in your group, brainstorm other ideas to go along with your assigned theme. When you've finished, write a brief letter to someone who has never heard of your assigned theme. Use your notes to help you write a clear, concise letter that will help that person begin to understand your theme.

Give groups a few minutes to read, jot down notes, and write their letters. Then have them share their letters with the class.

ASK • **How easy or difficult was it to explain your theme? Explain.**

Historical Context | Genesis 3:1-24

We have no way of knowing how much time passed between the completion of creation and the temptation described in Genesis 3:1-24. God seems not as concerned about telling us the chronology as he is about telling us what happened and its significance.

The first thing we read about is the craftiness of the serpent. Created good by God, somehow this creature was being used by Satan to deceive the first humans. Perhaps its craftiness was a natural trait, and Satan chose it for his use because of that.

The serpent's first question demonstrated his craftiness. He must have known what God had really commanded, but asking the question made Eve begin to think. She likely began to wonder, "Why did God let us eat from all the trees but this one?" The serpent, knowing he had made Eve question God, proceeded to take his deception further, suggesting that God had lied to her and insinuating that God didn't have Eve's best interests in mind. It must have made sense to Eve, because she took the bait and ate the fruit.

Sometimes people lay more blame on Eve than on Adam because she ate first. But in reality, more responsibility should fall on Adam because he had heard God speak the words of prohibition. He wasn't deceived by Satan's agent, the serpent. He simply took the fruit from Eve, apparently without much question. He should have known better.

As always, temptation promised more than the sin delivered. Adam and Eve didn't "become like God" but instead were hit in the face with reality: They had disobeyed God. Suddenly their nakedness, which had been natural when all was good, seemed so wrong. And as usually happens with us, one sin led to another: They decided to hide from God.

God had every right to be angry. Most of us would have been. The beings God had created and provided for so bountifully had turned against him. They had refused to trust God. But God came looking for them, knowing well what had happened. Here God showed his character and established what would become a pattern: When people sin and turn against God, God seeks them out and draws them to himself. God loves his people—no matter what.

God's constant love for us doesn't mean we can avoid the consequences of sin. The rest of this passage relates the consequences of Adam and Eve's sin, which from that point on fell upon all humanity. However, the banishing of Adam and Eve from the Garden (Genesis 3:22-24) was not so much for punishment as for their protection. Now that they had sinned, sin would be part of them as long as they lived. Should they eat of the tree of life in the Garden, they would live forever under the power of sin. Only physical death could save them from such a life of torture. And God had a plan to save them from spiritual death, a plan that likely is hinted at in Genesis 3:15: Jesus would come and experience death but defeat Satan forever!

Tip From the Trenches

The theological language in the book of Romans can be challenging for teenagers. But Romans 5:12-19 gives an excellent capsule statement about both the far-reaching effects of Adam's sin and the overwhelming grace of God's solution in Christ. Focus on those two points with your students, and don't get bogged down by the section about the law in verse 13.

- **How well do you think your letter would help someone understand why we sin?**

SAY **Now let's learn more about the relationship between our sin and God's great love for us.**

Contaminated by Sin

Distribute Bibles, and have students turn to **Genesis 3**. Enlist volunteers to read the following parts: the narrator (reads everything not in quotation marks), the serpent, the woman, the Lord God, and the man.

Have the volunteers read all of **Genesis 3** while others follow along.

SAY **We're going to illustrate this passage in a three-part story. You will work in a small group to examine part of the story and then illustrate it on poster board. You can use words, drawings, magazine pictures, or a combination.**

Form at least three groups of no more than four people each. Give each group pens and an "Exit From Eden" handout (p. 34). Assign each group one of the three sections on the handout to discuss. (If you have more than three groups, give some groups the same section but have them work separately.) Set out poster board, markers, old magazines, scissors, and glue.

When all the groups have completed their illustrations, call them together. Ask volunteers from the Conflict group and the Consequences group to share their work.

ASK
- **Why do you think God went so far as to banish Adam and Eve from the garden?**
- **How do you think Adam and Eve might have responded to their banishment from the garden?**

The Solution group will share its work later.

Purified by Christ

SAY **Sin always separates; just as conflict separated the characters in the opening skits, so the conflict between our sinfulness and God's holiness separates us from God. God is completely holy, and he cannot stand any sin. And when we sin, we are completely permeated by sin—let me show you.**

Fill a clear glass with water, and

SAY **The water in this glass represents Adam and Eve before they sinned.**

Swirl several drops of liquid food coloring into the water.

SAY **This food coloring represents Adam and Eve's sin. I need a volunteer to try to pour out only the clear water into the second glass.**

After the student tries,

ASK • **Why couldn't our volunteer pour out just the clear water?**

• **How is the way the food coloring affects the water like the way sin affects our lives?**

SAY **Just as it was impossible to pour out clear water after I'd put food coloring in the glass, it's impossible to find an uncontaminated, holy part of a person who has sinned.**

ASK • **Why do you think Adam and Eve's sin still has consequences in the world today?**

• **Why do *we* sin?**

SAY **The first sin not only contaminated Adam and Eve completely, it also contaminated the whole human race. The glass of water could stand for humanity, because the first sin tainted everyone still to be born.**

Have a volunteer read **Romans 3:23** aloud, and ask students to reflect silently on this question: "How is your life contaminated by sin?"

ASK • **How could the water in this glass be made clear again?**

Whether or not students come up with a workable solution, point out that Adam and Eve—and human beings today—were powerless to decontaminate themselves. But God is not powerless, and he presented a solution.

Invite volunteers from the Solution group to share their illustration. Line up all three illustrations, and

ASK • **What do you think it was like for God to see his beautiful world contaminated by sin?**

• **Which consequences of sin—your own personal consequences or the consequence of evil in the world—do you find most troubling?**

• **How can Jesus Christ take some of the pain out of those consequences?**

Pour the contaminated water into the bowl, and fill the glass with clear water.

Teacher Skillbuilder

Not every student who attends Sunday school or youth group is a Christian. You can be part of the process God uses to lead teenagers to himself when you offer a clear call to respond to Christ's gift of salvation. Some students may not know enough about the Gospel message to take that challenge; a good outline you can use is the "Romans Road" (Romans 3:10, 23; 5:8, 12; 6:23; and 10:9-10).

Bible Application

Bridging the Gap

Give students an opportunity to spend some time in quiet reflection. Ask them to sit with their eyes closed and think about the following Scripture passages and questions or statements that follow. Pause after each question or statement to allow students to reflect without answering aloud.

For Extra Impact

To encourage a reflective mood as students think about these questions, you may want to turn out overhead lights, light candles, and play soothing instrumental music.

Tip From the Trenches

To help strengthen the connection between church and home, photocopy the "Taking It Home" page at the end of this study, and either distribute copies to students before they leave or mail them home. Encourage students to complete the reading, activities, and discussion with their families during the coming week.

Read aloud **Genesis 3:8-9**, pause, and then

ASK • **Where are *you*? Are you walking with God, or are you hiding from him?**

Pause to give students time to think about their responses.

Read aloud **Genesis 3:10-11a**, pause, and then

ASK • **What have *you* been listening to when you thought you were out of God's sight? What lies have you believed?**

Pause to give students time to think about their responses.

Read aloud **Genesis 3:13**, pause, and then

ASK • **Are you ready to take responsibility for your actions, or are you too busy pointing fingers?**

Pause to give students time to think about their responses.

SAY **If you've found, in this quiet time in God's Word, that you have some sins you need to tell God about, go ahead. God knows them already, but he's waiting for you, ready to hear you say you're sorry. And if you've never gotten close enough to God to have that kind of conversation, you can start right now. Tell God that you know you are every bit as much a sinner as Adam and Eve, and ask Jesus to be the solution—to forgive your sins and bridge that separation between you and God. Begin your conversation with God by personalizing Romans 3:23: "God, I have sinned and fallen short of your glory."**

Allow a minute or two after the final statement, and then quietly tell kids that they may leave in silence whenever they are ready.

Faith Journal

Give students each an index card and a pen. Have teenagers write their names and answers to the following question on their index cards:

- How can knowing your amazing importance to God affect your actions and decisions?

Have teenagers return their index cards to you. Before you meet with the group again, take some time to write personal responses to your students on their index cards. You may want to keep a notebook or a box containing copies of these index cards.

For more information about the Faith Journal option, refer to page 5 in the Introduction.

Music Connection

idea:listen

Give each student a blank sheet of paper and a black marker, and have students each draw a big, black splotch somewhere on their papers. Point out that the splotches on their papers represent the times students have fallen short of God's glory.

track 3: Play the song "I Need You." As the song is playing, have students think of situations in their lives which match the situations discussed in the song—times they need God's love and forgiveness. When the song is finished,

ASK

- **What are some of the ways or reasons that we need God?**
- **Can you think of a time it might be hard to tell God that you need him? Explain.**
- **According to this song and the lesson today, how does God respond when we call on him and ask for his forgiveness?**

Have students throw away their papers and take clean sheets of paper as a reminder that God takes our sins away and gives us a "clean slate" when we tell him about our sins and ask for his forgiveness.

I Need You

(recorded by Mad at the World)

Every day's a day to start again-
To gather your thoughts; to walk away from sin.
If you don't succeed, then try and try again-
Fall on your knees, and start to pray again.

Chorus:
I need you.
I need you.
I need you.
I need you.

It's easy to feel like everything's a waste;
People are fighting, always so much haste.
All the time, there's someone loving you.
So don't fight his love; just let his love flow through.

Chorus:
I need it.
I need it.
I need it.
I need it.
I need it. (I need your love.)
I need it (from heaven above).
I need it. (I need your love.)
I need it.

I'm trying to love and be kind every day.
I know God is love, and love's the only way.
I never knew love like your love, it's for real.
I gave you my broken heart so it could heal.

Chorus:
I need it. (I need your love.)
I need it (from heaven above).
I need it. (I need your love.)
I need it.

I need your love
From heaven above.
I need it.
I need your love
From heaven above.
I need it.

[music]

searching

Exit From Eden

idea:sin

Conflict:

In your group, discuss the following questions:

- What do you think motivated Eve to disobey God?
- Why would she believe the serpent instead of God?
- Do you think Adam is less to blame than Eve? Explain.
- Who (or what) are some of the tempters we face today? Why do we give in to temptation?

- What lies do you think people fall for today? Why would they believe these lies?

Using the materials provided, illustrate the conflict in the Bible passage.

Consequences:

In your group, discuss the following questions:

- How did Adam and Eve's action affect:
- their view of themselves? (See **Genesis 3:7**.)
- their relationship with God?
- their relationship with each other?
- Describe how some of the consequences of sin listed in **Genesis 3:16-19** affect our lives and our world today.
- What consequences do you think Adam and Eve's action have on our relationship with God?

Using the materials provided, illustrate the consequences of sin.

Solution:

In your group, discuss the following questions:

- What hope for the future does God give? (See **Genesis 3:15**.) What does this mean? (See **Romans 16:20**.)
- Read **Romans 5:12-19** and write in your own words God's solution to the separation caused by sin.

Using the materials provided, illustrate God's solution.

[think]

stained

Talking About It | idea:discuss

Driving Home the Point:

"As I read and reread the great stories in the Bible it seems more and more clear that sin is separation from God, and one way to separate ourselves from God is to over-define God. If Jesus was like us, but sinless, it wasn't that he never did anything the moral majority of his day considered wrong. Indeed, he did many things that they considered sin, such as breaking the law by healing on the Sabbath. But he was never separate from the Source, while we, of our essence, separate ourselves over and over.

"The first great story in the Bible, after the wonderful paean of praise to Creation, is a story of separation from God, the story of Adam and Eve in the Garden. It doesn't really matter who was the first to eat of the fruit of the tree of the knowledge of good and evil. What is important is that in going against God's wishes, they separated themselves from their Maker. Both of them.

"Like many of the tales in Scripture, the story of the expulsion of the human beings from the Garden is an ambiguous one. It is a story not of punishment, but of separation, the two human beings' separation from God, and separation from their own natures."

(**Madeleine L'Engle,** *Glimpses of Grace*)

Talking At Home:

Read **Psalm 51:4** as a family and discuss these questions:

- What are ways that sin can cause separation from God?

- What can we as humans do about the sin that separates us from God?

Have you ever had a relationship become broken or strained because of a conflict? What did you do? Share your thoughts with your family.

Family Feud

Genesis 4:1-16

4

Cain Kills Abel

 **key question:** How should we treat our families?

 study focus: Teenagers will understand how poor choices can damage their relationships with God and with family members.

key verse: "Be devoted to one another in brotherly love. Honor one another above yourselves." Romans 12:10

A Look at the Study

Study Sequence	Minutes	What Students Will Do	Classroom Supplies
Getting Started	10 to 15	**Challenging Choices**—Think about how the choices they make affect members of their families.	Index cards, pens
Bible Story Exploration	10 to 15	**Cain's Choice**—Explore background information about the Cain and Abel story.	Bibles, "Historical Context" copies (p. 40), pens
	15 to 20	**Cause and Effect**—Experience the Bible story and explore the attitudes, emotions, and relationships of each character.	Bible, newsprint, tape, marker
Bible Application	5 to 10	**Fixer-Upper**—Commit to improving their relationships with family members.	Bibles, "And Behind Door Number One..." handouts (p. 44), pens
	up to 5	**Faith Journal**—Explore the Key Question and respond in writing.	Index cards, pens
Music Connection	5 to 10	**Trigger Happy**—Explore times they've responded in anger to unfair situations. Use this option at an appropriate time in the study.	CD: "Trigger Happy" (Track 4), CD player

Age-Level Insight

Becoming an independent, functioning human being is the great developmental task of growing up. This task comes to a head during adolescence. A teenager needs to determine a way to continue to be part of his or her family while becoming his or her own person. Parents and teenagers experience "bumps" along the path to accomplishing this. Remembering that God wants us to love our families can be difficult for young people at this stage of life. Putting those words into action can seem impossible sometimes. Provide teenagers with a safe place to talk about their struggles at home, and work hard to offer them practical, biblical advice.

Last Week's Impact

As teenagers arrive, greet them warmly and ask follow-up questions to review last week's study and Key Verse. Ask questions such as "What were some ideas your family had about repairing relationships that had been hurt by separations?" and "What kinds of separations did you discover between yourself and God?"

If you used the Faith Journal option last week, take this time to return your students' index cards to them.

Teacher Skillbuilder

Interactive learning occurs when students discuss and work cooperatively in pairs or small groups. This type of learning encourages students to work together, helps students feel better about themselves and get along well with others, and allows for new friendships to form outside of established cliques.

Getting Started

Challenging Choices

Give each student an index card and a pen.

SAY **I'd like you to think of a choice, either negative or positive, that you've been faced with in your life that would affect the members of your family in some way. An example might be the choice to drink and drive. When you've thought of a choice, write it on your index card.**

Have students form pairs, and tell partners to exchange index cards.

SAY **Now I'd like you to read your partner's card and think about ways that choice might affect members of your own family if you were faced with the choice. Write those ways on the other side of your partner's index card. Then, together with your partner, decide on the best course of action for each of your choices.**

Have pairs share the choices and the effects of those choices with the whole group.

Have pairs discuss these questions. After each question, ask pairs to report their answers to the whole group.

- **Describe a specific time you made a choice that affected members of your family negatively. What could you have done differently?**
- **Describe a specific time you made a choice that affected the members of your family positively. How did your family members react?**
- **Can you think of a time another member of your family made a choice that affected you negatively? Explain.**
- **How can the choices we make affect the way we treat our families?**

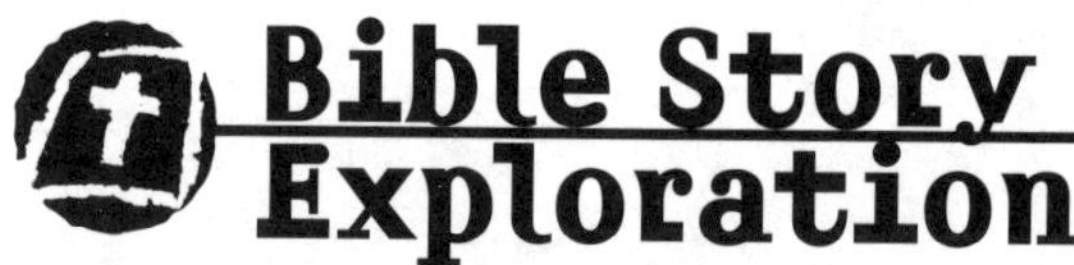

- **How does God want us to treat our families?**

Bible Story Exploration

Cain's Choice

Give each student a copy of the "Historical Context" box (p. 40), a Bible, and a pen.

SAY **I'd like you to begin your study of Cain and Abel by studying some background information. I'll give each pair a theme to research. As you read the information I've given you, I'd like**

you to be thinking about the theme I've assigned you. When you're finished reading, I'd like you to write a short narrative, or story, that tells about your assigned theme. Be thinking about how the characters might have been feeling in relation to your assigned theme.

To illustrate the fact that each of us makes critical decisions that can negatively or positively affect our relationships, show a brief clip of the video *Mr. Destiny*—the clip in which Mike shows Larry Burrows two trails of light in the air representing two opposite outcomes.

Assign pairs the following themes (it's OK if more than one pair has the same theme or if not all the themes are used):

- Love
- Hate
- Forgiveness
- Punishment
- Protection
- Sacrifice

Invite students to include information from the Bible story.

Give pairs a few minutes to read the information and write their narratives, and then have them present the narratives to the whole class.

ASK • **What does this information tell you about God?**

• **How do you think God wants us to treat our families, according to the information you just discovered?**

SAY **Let's learn more about the first family in the Bible.**

Cause and Effect

Tape a long sheet of newsprint to a wall. Use a marker to divide and label the sheet according to the diagram.

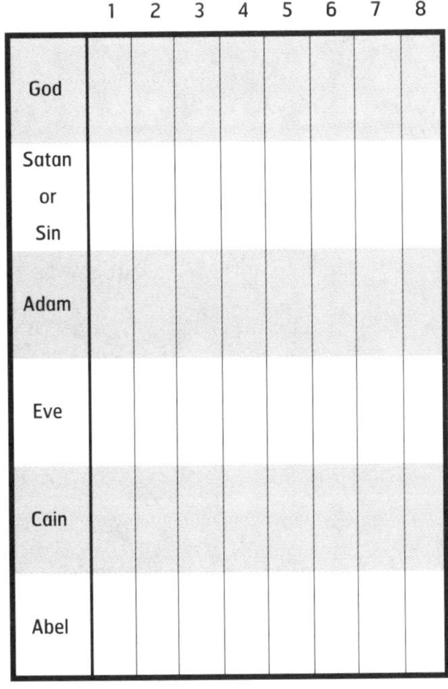

Have students form six groups (a group can be one person), and assign one of the following characters to each group: God, Satan or Sin, Adam, Eve, Cain, and Abel. Give each group a marker.

SAY **I'm going to read the story of Cain and Abel aloud. At certain points in the story, I'll pause. When I pause, I'd like you to decide with your group what choice (if any) your character made in that section. Some of your characters may not be mentioned directly, so you may need to use your imaginations. Then discuss the attitudes, emotions, and actions you think your character had at that point in the story. I'd also like your group to decide how your character's relationships were with each of the other characters at that point in the story. Rate each relationship on a scale of one to ten (with ten being the best). Each group will come up with five different ratings for each section (one for each relationship). Then choose one person in your group to jot down a few words describing the choice made and the attitudes, emotions, and actions in the correct column and to write each character's rating in the row next to that character's name.**

For example, if your group's character was Cain, for each story segment, you would first discuss and write down the attitudes, emotions, and actions your character had. Then you would think about what Cain's relationships might have been like with each of the other characters in the story at that point. Then you would rate each relationship from one to ten and write each rating in that character's box. For example, if you felt that Cain's relationship with Abel was pretty good, you'd write a seven in Abel's box for that story segment.

Read through the passage as follows:

SAY **Now Abel kept flocks, and Cain worked the soil. In the course of time Cain brought some of the fruits of the soil as an offering to the Lord. But Abel brought fat portions from**

Historical Context | Genesis 4:1-16

Cain and Abel, the first two humans born on earth, chose different occupations. Adam had likely done both occupations; each of his sons chose to specialize. This early in human history, we see that God created people to be different—to have different interests and skills. It's interesting, though, that Abel's choice of lifestyle was likely a contemplative one. Herding animals gave him a lot of time to think and reflect on what God had done. Later in Scripture, we see several other prominent thinkers who were animal caretakers—Abraham, Moses, and David, to name a few.

Some have suggested that God accepted Abel's sacrifice because it involved the shedding of blood and rejected Cain's because it didn't. However, nothing God had told humans to that point required blood sacrifice. It's more likely that God accepted or rejected the sacrifices based on the attitude of the heart. Abel's sacrifice came from true gratitude for what God had done for him; Cain's apparently came from a feeling of obligation to maintain God's favor. Abel offered the best he had; Cain offered simply a sampling of his fruits. God wants our best, and he wants our hearts to be right.

God knew Cain was at a dangerous junction. In Genesis 4:7, God's response to Cain was a loving warning—be careful what you do; sin can get the best of you. Unfortunately, Cain's jealousy got the best of him, and he kept going in the direction God already knew he had been heading. The evil started by Adam and Eve would continue. Cain proceeded with his planned deception and murdered his younger brother, Abel.

God did not question Cain after the murder in order to gain information. By engaging Cain with such a question, God was offering him a chance to admit his sin and repent. As with Adam and Eve, Cain's sin in killing Abel was followed by a second sin: lying to God. God's second question was one of accusation, encouraging Cain to consider what he had done. When God said, "Your brother's blood cries out to me," the word for blood is plural—indicating the inclusion of Abel's would-have-been offspring in the cry. Abel's premature death snuffed out an entire line of descendants, and God was holding Cain responsible.

When God pronounced judgment upon Cain for his sin, Cain finally came to his senses and realized that separation from God would mean his own death. As with Adam and Eve, God was merciful, providing protection for Cain even though he didn't deserve it.

Jealousy and sin ripped apart the family of Adam and Eve. Yet this was the family through whom God would work to populate the earth. God must have known from the beginning what a sinful bunch these humans would be, yet he loved them just the same. And that's a very comforting message for human beings today.

some of the firstborn of his flock. [Pause.] **The Lord looked with favor on Abel and his offering, but on Cain and his offering he did not look with favor. So Cain was very angry, and his face was downcast.** [Pause.] **Then the Lord said to Cain, "Why are you angry? Why is your face downcast? If you do what is right, will you not be accepted? But if you do not do what is right, sin is crouching at your door; it desires to have you, but you must master it."** [Pause.] **Now Cain said to his brother Abel, "Let's go out to the field." And while they were in the field, Cain attacked his brother Abel and killed him.** [Pause.] **Then the Lord said to Cain, "Where is your brother Abel?" "I don't know," he replied. "Am I my brother's keeper?"** [Pause.] **The Lord said, "What have you done? Listen! Your brother's blood cries out to me from the ground. Now you are under a curse and driven from the ground, which opened its mouth to receive your brother's blood from your hand. When you work the ground, it will no longer yield its crops for you. You will be a restless wanderer on the earth."** [Pause.] **Cain said to the Lord, "My punishment is more than I can bear. Today you are driving me from the land, and I will be hidden from your presence; I will be a restless wanderer on the earth, and whoever finds me will kill me."** [Pause.] **But the Lord said to him, "Not so; if anyone kills Cain, he will suffer vengeance seven times over." Then the Lord put a mark on Cain so that no one who found him would kill him. So Cain went out from the Lord's presence and lived in the land of Nod, east of Eden.**

Give groups a few minutes to share what they wrote on the chart.

ASK
- **At what points along Cain's journey did he make choices that affected the direction of his life?**
- **How did each consecutive choice affect Cain's relationships with his family?**
- **How do you think things would have been different if Cain had made a different choice somewhere along the way?**
- **How do you think the way Cain felt compares to the way you felt in the experience you shared at the beginning of class?**

- **How do you think God wanted the members of Cain's family to treat each other?**

Bible Application

Fixer-Upper

SAY **God warned Cain that if he made poor choices, sin would be like a wild animal, waiting outside his door to pounce on him**

for Younger teenagers

Assign groups to each of the six characters and say: **As I read the story, I'd like you to listen for the attitudes and emotions your character might have been feeling during each section, as well as what your character's relationships would have been like with the other characters. When I call out "Freeze!" I'd like you to first move into a position that demonstrates how close your character's relationships with the other characters might be. For example, if your group's character is Cain and you feel that Cain is really not close to Abel, your group would move as far away from the Abel group as possible. Once you've moved, I'd like you to freeze in a position that you think demonstrates the way your character might have been thinking and feeling at that point. For example, if you think your character might have been sad, you might make a sad face and hunch over.**
Read the sections of the story and yell "Freeze!" after each one. After students have frozen into position, have each group explain why it chose the position it did.

(Genesis 4:7). Cain's biggest failure came in the way he responded to a member of his own family. Sin attacked him in the place he was most vulnerable.

ASK
- **Do you think you are more vulnerable to sin's attacks with your own family members? Why or why not?**
- **How do you think Satan might take advantage of this vulnerability?**

- **How can negative reactions to family members harm your relationship with God?**

Give each student the "And Behind Door Number One..." handout (p. 44), a Bible, and a pen. Allow five minutes for your teenagers to complete the handout.

Have students form pairs, and have partners read the Key Verse together and discuss how it relates to dealing with sins that are "crouching at the doors" in their homes. Ask partners to share prayer requests with each other for improving their family relationships.

Faith Journal

Give students each an index card and a pen. Have teenagers write their names and answers to the following question on their index cards:

- How do you think the choices you make in your own life affect members of your family?

Have teenagers return their index cards to you. Before you meet with the group again, take some time to write personal responses to your students on their index cards. You may want to keep a notebook or a box containing copies of these index cards.

For more information about the Faith Journal option, refer to page 5 in the Introduction.

Tip From the Trenches

You'll need to be sensitive to the fact that families sometimes have "secrets," such as sexual or physical abuse, that occur behind closed doors. Be prepared to offer support and assistance to students who may be the victims in destructive family relationships. If you suspect a teenager is being abused, talk to him or her privately and let him or her know that you need to report to the Christian education director or the pastor.

Tip From the Trenches

To help strengthen the connection between church and home, photocopy the "Taking It Home" page at the end of this study, and either distribute copies to students before they leave or mail them home. Encourage students to complete the reading, activities, and discussion with their families during the coming week.

Music Connection

[mu/Sic]

idea:listen

Have students form pairs and share situations in which they or people they know have responded in anger or violence to difficult or unfair circumstances. (For example, someone might say, "My dad tailgated someone who cut him off on the highway.")

track 4:
Then play the song "Trigger Happy." While the song is playing, have students identify other possible violent or angry reactions as well as alternate responses to negative situations. After the song,

ASK
- **What are some of the negative reactions you heard or came up with in your pairs?**
- **How do these reactions compare to Cain's reaction in the lesson?**
- **What are some better reactions to difficult situations?**
- **How can the ways we react in difficult situations affect the members of our families?**

Trigger Happy

(recorded by Insyderz)

Man, this world's goin' down the tubes
With gangs and guns and drug abuse.
For the moment, whatcha got to lose—
Extend a hand, do what you can do.

This is my cry, this is my plea
To make a better society
Do you want to see inside of me?
Wake up and smell the coffee.

Chorus:
Any punk can point and pull the trigger,
But it takes a real man to bite your lip and to take a stand (yeah).
Any punk can point and pull the trigger;
To walk away is a loss of pride, but at least you're still alive.

Gotta act big, gotta stare me down.
You're actin' stupid like a drunken clown.
You could be foolin', maybe jokin' around—
Someday your jokes will put you in the ground.

Lord, oh please, I'm so confused—
Why do they do what they do?
Why can't they focus more on you?
They are blind to the truth.

Chorus (repeat twice)

Put down your guard, let your fists relax;
Don't need your boys to get your back.
Say something nice, don't always attack—
No one gets hurt, no one gets whacked.

Change your style, and you will see—
It's much better in unity.
No more violence, no more pain—
Jesus saves from goin' down the drain.

And Behind Door Number One...

idea:family

[t h i n k]

home

Draw an outline of the rooms in your house with a space left between the rooms to represent the doorways.

1. Place an X beside the doorway in each room where you are often involved in family conflict.
2. Picture who the conflict is usually with and how it occurs.
3. Ask yourself if your own poor choices, in any way, contribute to the conflict. If so, what might God be trying to tell you right now?
4. Which of your family relationships need the most work?
5. Read **Romans 12:10**, and write how this verse applies to one of your family relationships. Commit this verse to memory, and let it serve as a prayer to God for your relationship with this family member.
6. Now erase the X on your paper, and draw a cross there to symbolize a new way of relating with Jesus' help.
7. Write a short letter to the family member you chose, sharing the discoveries you've made with him or her. Share the commitment you're making to make the relationship better, and ask him or her to make a similar commitment. Close with a prayer, asking God to help the two of you strengthen your relationship. Share your letter with the family member you chose.

Driving Home the Point:

"A family was involved in a serious traffic accident. Mike, the youngest of two brothers involved, was badly injured and needed a blood transfusion. Mike's big brother Danny, who was only eight years old, had the same blood type as his younger brother. The dad sat down with Danny and carefully explained to him why this blood transfusion was needed and how wonderful it would be for his little brother. After some silence, Danny responded by saying, 'Yes, Daddy, I'll give my blood to Mike so he can get well.'

"At the hospital, a pint of blood was drawn from Danny's veins. Only after the needle was removed did Danny turn to his father with tears rolling down his cheeks and ask, 'Daddy, when do I die?'

The father suddenly realized with a shock that Danny had misunderstood his explanation of giving blood. Danny thought he was giving all of his blood to save the life of his brother! He thought that he would die after the transfusion was over. Yet he still had agreed to help his little brother."

(**Wayne Rice**, Hot Illustrations for Youth Talks)

Talking At Home:

Read the "love chapter" **(1 Corinthians 13)** together and discuss these questions:

- What do you think would happen if you treated each other according to the advice given in this chapter?

- What are some practical ways you could live out the words in this chapter in your family life?

Take a moment, and think silently about one family member with whom you would like to have a better relationship. Then meet with that person (maybe over coffee or soft drinks), and discuss ways you could improve your relationship (you may want to use **1 Corinthians 13** as a guide).
You might agree to keep one another accountable (gently, of course!) for new behaviors. You could also agree to pray together about your relationship.

To Obey or Not to Obey

Genesis 6:5-22

5

Noah Builds an Ark

key question: What does it mean to obey God?

study focus: Teenagers will understand that their obedience to God can serve as an excellent opportunity to share their faith.

key verse: "Peter and the other apostles replied: 'We must obey God rather than men!'" Acts 5:29

A Look at the Study

Study Sequence	Minutes	What Students Will Do	Classroom Supplies
Getting Started	5 to 10	**Who's the Boss?**—Identify who they're obedient to and how they decide whether to be obedient.	Chalkboard, chalk
Bible Story Exploration	5 to 10	**Noah's Obedience**—Explore background information about Noah's building of the Ark.	Bibles, "Historical Context" copies (p. 50), pens, paper
	10 to 15	**A Modern Noah**—Experience what it must have been like to build the ark from several different points of view.	Bibles, "Ark-Building Checklist" handouts (p. 54), scissors, paper, pens
	10 to 15	**Noah's Voice Mail**—Imagine what Noah's family and friends thought while he was building the ark.	"Voice Mail" copies (p. 56)
Bible Application	10 to 15	**Obedience Options**—Explore ways their own obedience to God might present opportunities to share their faith with others.	Bibles, index cards, pens
	up to 5	**Faith Journal**—Explore the Key Question and respond in writing.	Index cards, pens
Music Connection	5 to 10	**Used**—Explore what it means to obey God. Use this option at an appropriate time in the study.	"Used" lyric copies (p. 53), pens, CD: "Used" (Track 5), CD player

Age-Level Insight

Teenagers don't always see the importance of obedience to parents, to teachers, to the law, or to God. Often they see rules and laws as impediments to all the things they want to do and the fun they want to have. Sometimes teenagers have a hard time understanding that laws and rules were made to benefit them and others, not to limit them.

Explore with your students the ways God asks his people to obey, and work with them to help them understand that these rules were created for their benefit. Help them to understand all of the implications of obedience vs. disobedience.

Getting Started

Who's the Boss?

Begin by asking teenagers to raise their hands if someone told them what to do this week. Have students call out the position each authority figure had while you write their answers on the chalkboard. (Some examples are a teacher, a parent, or a coach.) After you have finished writing all their answers, ask students to refer to the list as they discuss the following questions in pairs. Have each pair report its answer back to the whole group after each question.

ASK
- **Who has the right to tell you what to do? Why?**
- **How do you usually react when someone tells you what to do? Give examples.**
- **Why is it often difficult to take orders?**
- **Is it always necessary to understand why you are told to do something before you obey?**
- **How do you decide if and when you are going to obey someone else?**

?
- **How do you decide if and when you're going to obey God?**

SAY **It sometimes can be difficult to obey someone else. We may not always understand why an authority figure asks us to do something. Today we're going to explore what it means to obey God, even when we don't understand his plan entirely.**

Last Week's Impact

As teenagers arrive, greet them warmly and ask follow-up questions to review last week's study and Key Verse. Ask questions such as "How do the choices you make affect members of your family?" and "Are you working on improving a relationship with a member of your family? If so, how?"

If you used the Faith Journal option last week, take this time to return your students' index cards to them.

Teacher Skillbuilder

Teenagers sometimes have a difficult time obeying authority. Help them to understand and respect your authority by setting clear, consistent expectations, helping students to understand the reasons behind those expectations, and expecting (and trusting) students to live up to your expectations.

Bible Story Exploration

Noah's Obedience

Give each student a copy of the "Historical Context" box (p. 50), a Bible, a blank piece of paper, and a pen.

SAY **I'd like you to begin your study of the story of Noah's Ark by studying some background information.**

Assign each pair one of these characters: God or Noah.

SAY
- **Each pair is going to act as a newscasting team. I'd like you to read the information I've given you. When you're finished reading, I'd like you to answer the following questions about your character that you've found in the information you've read.**

- **Who?**
- **What?**
- **Where?**
- **When?**
- **Why?**
- **How?**

Make sure to include any important information as you answer these questions. Then use the information you've gathered to write a news release that you will share "on the air."

Invite students to take their research further by including information from the Bible story.

Give pairs a few minutes to read the information and write their news releases, and then have them present the news releases to the whole class.

ASK • **What does this information tell you about God?**

- **What does the information tell you about humans?**

- **According to your research, what do you think it means to obey God?**

SAY **Let's learn more about Noah's obedience to God.**

Use the "Souvenir Stand" video segment of *Shock Wave: Volume 1* (available from Group Publishing) for a different perspective on the building of the ark.

A Modern Noah

Have your students form three groups. Cut apart the "Ark-Building Checklist" handout (p. 54), and give each group a handout section, Bibles, a piece of paper, and a pen. Ask each group to choose a recorder to record the group's work.

SAY **Imagine that we're alive during the time of Noah. Read your section and your Scripture passage carefully, and try to put yourselves in the shoes of the person you have been assigned. Use your imagination and any information you can find in your Scripture passage to help you complete your assignment.**

Allow five minutes for each group to complete its assignment. After the groups are finished, have a spokesperson from each group read the group's handout section and share the completed assignment with the rest of the group.

ASK • **How difficult were these things for Noah to complete?**

- **Why did God choose to use Noah?**
- **How do you think Noah must have felt to be the only person choosing to follow God's commands?**
- **Have you ever been in a situation in which you were the only person choosing to live by God's standards? If so, how did it feel?**

for Younger teenagers

You may want to move from group to group to see how younger teenagers are doing on the assignment. If a group is having trouble getting started, ask some starter questions. Have students put themselves in the shoes of the person they are pretending to be. Help them to see how they can include the facts they learn about Noah from the Scripture passage in their report.

Historical Context | Genesis 6:5-22

The sin begun by Adam and Eve, and then continued by Cain and their other offspring, must have multiplied even more in the generations that followed. The sin became so great, in fact, that the Bible describes the heart of humanity as "evil all the time" and states that God was grieved by what humans had become. The pain described in Genesis 6:6 could mean either physical pain or emotional sorrow, but in either case it was severe.

God's statement in Genesis 6:7 may seem as if it stemmed from anger or a desire for revenge, but instead it grew out of his pain and was a sorrowful acknowledgement that to make things better, most of the earth's population would have to die. The people that God had created had so turned against him that he had to start over with the few who remained faithful.

Fortunately, one righteous man still loved God. The word translated "righteous" in verse 9 indicates that Noah sought both to worship and obey God and also to live in fairness with his human neighbors who didn't share his values. Also, the statement that he was blameless indicates a moral purity. Noah was a shining example of goodness in a dark world.

Consider the immensity of the task Noah undertook. The ark was half again the length of a football field, as wide as a basketball court is long, and as tall as a five-story building. There were to be three decks inside and many rooms to house all the different animals. All of this was to be built of a particular kind of wood (which we can't identify precisely) in an arid area where wood was not likely plentiful. And Noah had probably never seen more water than that in a small stream.

Obviously no one had ever built a floating zoo of that size. Fortunately, God knew what he was doing. Modern shipbuilding experts have confirmed that the dimensions given in the Bible would be ideal to ensure that a large wooden vessel would remain intact and upright while adrift in heavy seas.

This flood was to be one of a kind. The Hebrew word used here was apparently coined specifically to describe what happened. It is used only here, in Psalm 29:10, and in Isaiah 54:9. All likely refer to this same incident.

In addition to caring for his family, Noah was given the responsibility of housing and feeding two of every kind of animal in the ark (Genesis 6:19, 21). But he didn't have to go round them up. In an amazing miracle, God led all those animals to the ark at just the right time. And the reason there were seven pairs of certain animals was so that Noah would have animals to sacrifice in worship without wiping out a species (Genesis 7:2-3).

We don't know how often Noah was discouraged. We don't know if his neighbors ridiculed him, but we assume they must have. We don't know if Noah's family thought he had lost his mind. But we do know that "he did everything just as God commanded him." And that's a great example of faithful obedience for all of us.

- **Do you ever feel like just going along with the crowd? Why or why not?**

- **What does it mean to obey God?**

Noah's Voice Mail

SAY **I'd like you to imagine what it might have been like if Noah had an answering machine during the time he was building the ark.** Assign each student one of the following parts: Noah, Ralph, Rhoda, Jarad, Noah's mother-in-law, the answering machine beep, the thunder, the rain, and the dial tone. (If you have more students than parts, assign more than one student to the thunder and the rain. If you have fewer students than parts, assign some students more than one part.) Give each student a copy of the "Voice Mail" page (p. 56), and have students read through the script.

ASK
- **Why do you think God didn't simply provide an ark for Noah?**
- **How do you think Noah felt about his assignment?**
- **Just think of the attention that must have come from constructing this massive boat. Do you think God planned on people noticing what Noah was doing? Why or why not?**

- **How did Noah's obedience to God affect his friends and family?**

Bible Application

Obedience Options

SAY **When God asked Noah to spend years building an ark, it probably seemed foolish. Yet Noah's obedience caused him to stand out and be noticed by people who didn't believe in God. Because of his obedience, Noah was able to share his faith with the people around him.**

Have your students form groups of three. Ask them to discuss the following questions:

- **Has living an obedient lifestyle to God ever caused people who don't follow God to notice you or ridicule you? Explain.**
- **Noah's obedience served as an opportunity for him to share God's plan with his neighbors. How might God want you to turn criticism from others into an opportunity to communicate about God with them?**

Give each trio Bibles, index cards, and pens.

SAY **I'd like you, in your trio, to take a few minutes to think of possible scenarios in which you may receive criticism or questions from others about your obedience to God. One example might be the pressure from friends to cheat on a test because "everyone else is." Think of as many scenarios as you can, and write each one on a separate index card.**

Give trios a few minutes to do this and then have each trio look up the Key Verse.

SAY **Now I'd like you to choose three of your scenarios. For each**

for Younger teenagers

To provide younger teenagers a more active response to this study, assign each trio one of the following scenarios in which criticism and questions from others about obedience to God may present opportunities to share faith:

- Your friends are pressuring you to cheat on a test.
- Your brother or sister asks you to sneak out of the house after curfew with him or her.
- Your friends ask you why you never use bad language.
- Your friends ask you to go on an overnight trip with no adult supervision.

Have students answer these questions in their trios:

- **How could you obey God in this situation?**
- **How might your obedience to God in this situation give you a chance to tell other people about God?**

Give trios a few minutes to create short role plays that demonstrate ways they can turn criticism and questions from others into opportunities to share their faith. Have them use the Key Verse at least once in their role plays. After a few minutes, have trios present their role plays to the whole group.

scenario, you'll need to brainstorm possible responses you could make to the criticism or questions. Try to come up with responses that would allow you to share your faith. I'd like you to use the Key Verse in your responses, either word-for-word or paraphrased. Write your responses on the backs of your index cards.

Give trios a few minutes to do this and then have them share their scenarios and responses with the large group.

SAY **Sometimes obeying God means putting words together with your actions. I'd like you to close your eyes and take a moment in silence to talk to God about one specific way you can be God's spokesperson this week.**

Allow a minute of silence, and then quietly tell students they can leave when they are ready.

Faith Journal

Give students each an index card and a pen. Have teenagers write their names and answers to the following question on their index cards:

- How do you think your obedience to God, even in times of pressure, might affect people around you?

Have teenagers return their index cards to you. Before you meet with the group again, take some time to write personal responses to your students on their index cards. You may want to keep a notebook or a box containing copies of these index cards.

For more information about the Faith Journal option, refer to page 5 in the Introduction.

For Extra Impact

Collect enough used spark plugs from a local mechanic to give one to each student. Tell students that in order for a car to run properly, there must be an electrical arc that moves in the gap in the spark plug. Ask students to keep the spark plugs with them this week as reminders that when they obey God with both their actions and their words, they can be the "arcs" that God uses to show his love to the people around them.

Tip From the Trenches

To help strengthen the connection between church and home, photocopy the "Taking It Home" page at the end of this study, and either distribute copies to students before they leave or mail them home. Encourage students to complete the reading, activities, and discussion with their families during the coming week.

Music Connection

[mu/Sic]

idea:listen

Give each student a copy of the lyrics for "Used" and a pen.

track 5:
Play the song. As you play it, have students listen for ways that they believe the song demonstrates what it means to obey God as well as things they feel are *not* what God asks of us as his children. Have them circle the things that demonstrate what it means to obey God and underline the things that aren't what God asks of us. After the song,

ASK

- **What things in the song do you feel demonstrate what it means to obey God?**
- **How do you think Noah and his family did these things in the Bible story?**
- **What things in the song do you feel aren't what God asks of us?**
- **Do you think that God "uses" us or "makes us give up our lives for him"? Explain.**
- **What did God want from Noah? What does God want from us?**

Used

(recorded by Glisten)

I've made my skin become a home for you,
And all I do will glorify your name.
I've made myself become a pawn for you;
So move me, Lord, on this chessboard of life.

You've made me into your vessel, Lord.
You've filled me up; now pour me out.
You've made me give up my life for you,
And is that the least that I could do?

I've made my skin become a home for you,
And all I do will glorify your name.
I've made myself become a pawn for you;
Is that the least that I could do?

All I do will glorify
All I do will glorify
All I do will glorify your name.

I've made my skin become a home for you
(glorify).
I've made myself become a pawn for you
(glorify).

[music]

obedience

Ark-Building Checklist

idea:abilities

[t h i n k]

Job Reference

Character of Noah (Genesis 6:5-12)
Your friend Noah recently applied for a job at Boats-R-Us construction school. He asked you for a personal letter of reference to help him get accepted into the school. Write a letter of reference telling everything you know about his character and work ethic. In your letter, you may want to contrast him with other people around him.

Ark Blueprints

Construction of the Ark (Genesis 6:13-16)
You're an instructor at Boats-R-Us construction school. Recently Mr. Noah, one of your students, submitted plans for his final project. He intends to build an ark. You are required to grade his proposal. You believe that perhaps Mr. Noah has made a mistake with his dimensions. After describing the size of his flotation device in practical terms, please submit a written evaluation of Mr. Noah's ark using the following criteria: seaworthiness, maneuverability, practical usefulness, and possibility of completion.

qualify

Credit Check

Covenant From God (Genesis 6:17-21)
You're a supplier for the Mediterranean Lumber Company. Recently you received an extremely large order for cypress wood and tar from a local man named Noah. When you inquired about his ability to pay for the lumber, he referred you to his boss. Write your recommendation about whether you think giving Noah the lumber is a good risk. Be sure to include the following in your evaluation: your opinion about his boss' ability to pay back the loan, what the lumber will be used for, whether Noah has any collateral in case he is unable to make payments, and what you would recommend as a reasonable timetable for repayment considering Noah's intended use for the materials.

Driving Home the Point:

"Slowly I have realized that I do not have to be qualified to do what I am asked to do, that I just have to go ahead and do it, even if I can't do it as well as I think it ought to be done. This is one of the most liberating lessons of my life.

"The qualifications needed for God's work are very different from those of the world. In fact, when we begin to think we are qualified, we have already fallen for the tempter's wiles. Not one of us has to be qualified in order to employ lesson, meditation, and orison; to read, think, and pray over Scripture. We do not need to have gone to a theological seminary, or to have taken courses in Bible in or out of college. We do have to be willing to open ourselves to the power of the living Word. And sometimes that can be frightening."

(**Madeleine L'Engle,** *Glimpses of Grace*)

Talking At Home:

Discuss these questions as a family:

- Do you think Noah felt qualified to do what God asked of him?
- What "qualifications" did Noah need to fulfill the will of God?
- What qualifications do we need to fulfill the will of God?

Read **Psalm 86:11** together and discuss these questions:

- What does it mean to have an undivided heart?
- In what ways did Noah show that his heart was undivided?
- In what ways could you show that your heart is undivided?

Have you ever been ridiculed or put down for doing what you knew was right? What happened? Share those situations with the members of your family. How do you think God might use your obedience to him in the lives of other people?

Voice Mail

[NOAH] Hello, this is the Noah family. We're all busy, and we can't get to the phone right now. At the beep, please leave a message. We'll get back to you as soon as we can.

Beep

[RALPH] Noah, this is your neighbor, Ralph. Pick up the phone, will ya? What are you makin' such a big mess in your back yard for? You'd better clean it up before I call the city inspector.

Beep

[JARAD] Hey, Noah, this is your cousin, Jarad. I heard you have a huge workout facility under construction. Sounds like a great moneymaking plan. Can you cut me in on it? After all, we are family.

Beep

[RHODA] Noah, Noah, Noah. This is Rhoda. Have you flipped your lid? I heard you've been speaking to God lately. I'm saying this as a friend: Don't be such a fanatic.

Beep

[MOTHER-IN-LAW] So what are you, Noah, the weatherman? Predictin' rain in the middle of the desert? I knew my daughter shouldn't have married you. You jerk!

Beep

[RALPH] Noah, this is Ralph again. Who do you think you are to judge us? You build a big wooden box in your back yard, and suddenly you're better than everyone else. That thing is not a pulpit, you know. So stop your preaching.

Beep

[MOTHER-IN-LAW] *(faint sounds of* **Thunder** *in the background)* So what, now you're a veterinarian? My daughter told me you heard from God about collectin' animals. She said God told you, "If you build it, they will come." Come on, you numbskull. I knew my sweet little daughter shouldn't have married you. What kind of wild mushrooms have you been eatin', anyway? And enough with the God stuff already!

Beep

[JARAD] *(sounds of* **Thunder** *and* **Rain** *getting louder in the background)* Noah? Jarad again. All right, Noah, that's it. The family's disowning you. And if you think that we're all gonna stop enjoying life and huddle up in that little sweatbox of yours just because you had a message from God, you've got another think coming. A few drops of rain never hurt anybody. Now, why don't you get out of that overgrown crate and get a life? You're a disgrace!

Beep

[RHODA] *(sounds of loud* **Thunder** *and* **Rain** *in the background)* Noah? Noah, I know you're there. This is your old buddy, Rhoda. Come on, Noah, pick up the phone, will you? Pleeease? It's really starting to get deep out here...*(sound of the* ***Dial Tone****.)*

Promises, Promises

Genesis 7:1–8:22; 9:8-16

6

God Floods the Earth

 **key question:** How reliable are God's promises?

 **study focus:** Teenagers will see that God's promises are perfect and just.

key verse: "The Lord is faithful to all his promises and loving toward all he has made." Psalm 145:13b

A Look at the Study

Study Sequence	Minutes	What Students Will Do	Classroom Supplies
Getting Started	5 to 10	**Difficult Decisions**—Determine how they would decide whom to save on the Titanic, and then compare the experience to God's justice.	Bible
Bible Story Exploration	5 to 10	**The Flood**—Explore background information about God's flooding of the earth.	"Historical Context" copies (p. 60), poster board, markers
	10 to 15	**The Ark of God's Mercy**—Experience the story of the Ark by imagining they were there.	Bible, spray bottle filled with water, two cookie sheets, fan
Bible Application	10 to 15	**God's Promises**—Create their own parables expressing the reliability of God's promises.	Paper, pens
	5 to 10	**A God of Justice and Grace**—Examine a comparison of the flood to Christ's death on the cross and discover how the concept applies to their lives.	Bibles, "Hanging in the Balance" handouts (p. 64), pens
	up to 5	**Faith Journal**—Explore the Key Question and respond in writing.	Index cards, pens
Music Connection	5 to 10	**Never Forsaken**—Explore God's promises to them. Use this option at an appropriate time in the study.	Index cards, pens, CD: "Never Forsaken" (Track 6), CD player

Age-Level Insight

Teenagers can begin to explore the nuances of faithfulness. They can talk about and discover what commitment truly is. Help them discover that because God is faithful and keeps all his promises, his people are to be faithful and keep all their promises, too. Help teenagers see the broader implications of faithfulness in the areas of family, relationships, and vocation, and use this to help them become adults who are faithful to their commitments and promises.

Getting Started

Difficult Decisions

Begin by asking how many of your students know the story of the Titanic. Have students form groups of five and discuss this scenario:

Suppose only one six-passenger lifeboat was left on the Titanic and hundreds of people were still on the ship, about to drown. If you were the one person with the authority to decide who should be allowed to board the lifeboat, what criteria would you use to decide?

Tell your students that the ship is about to sink. They have exactly three minutes to agree on how they will decide who gets to live. (For example, they might choose a pregnant woman over a woman who is not pregnant, or they might choose an older, wiser person over a younger one.) When time is up, allow a spokesperson from each group to tell the group's decision and explain its rationale.

ASK

- **Was it difficult for your group to agree on how you would decide who lived? Why or why not?**
- **How did it feel to decide the fate of other people?**
- **How might you have felt differently if this were really happening?**
- **If you were one of the people left on the ship, would you trust someone else to decide whether you should be chosen to go on the lifeboat? Why or why not?**
- **Do you think God is ever in a position in which he has to decide which people to rescue and which people not to rescue? Explain.**

Read aloud **Ecclesiastes 3:17.**

ASK

- **What do you think this verse tells us about God's promises?**

Bible Story Exploration

The Flood

Set out pieces of poster board or newsprint and markers. Have students form pairs or trios, and give each group a copy of the "Historical Context" box (p. 60).

Last Week's Impact

As teenagers arrive, greet them warmly and ask follow-up questions to review last week's study and Key Verse. Ask questions such as "Did your obedience to God give you opportunities to share your faith this week? If so, how?" and "What did you learn with your family about having an undivided heart?"

If you used the Faith Journal option last week, take this time to return your students' index cards to them.

for Younger teenagers

You may want to move from group to group to see how younger teenagers are doing on the assignment. If a group is having trouble getting started, ask some starter questions, such as "Which people do you think are most important?" and "Which people do you think deserve to be saved the most?" Have students put themselves in the shoes of the people whose fates they are deciding.

For Extra Impact

If you want to add some mood music, you could play the soundtrack from the movie *Titanic* while the groups are working.

SAY **I'd like you to begin your exploration of the story of the Flood by learning and teaching each other some historical background information. I'm going to assign each group one paragraph from the "Historical Context" box. In your group, you'll need to read the information and decide on the main idea of your paragraph. Then you'll need to think of an image that portrays your main idea. When you've thought of an image, create a storyboard by drawing that image on poster board** [or newsprint]. **Make sure that everyone in your group is involved in the creation of your storyboard.**

Assign one pair or trio the first paragraph, one pair or trio the second paragraph, and so on. If you don't have enough pairs or trios to cover all the paragraphs, assign some groups more than one. Give groups a few minutes to read their information and create their storyboards. Then have groups share their storyboards with the whole class, one at a time.

After they're finished,

ASK
- **What was one interesting fact you learned from another group's presentation?**
- **What does the information you just learned about tell you about God?**
- **What does the information tell you about the reason God flooded the earth?**

- **Based on the information you just learned, do you think God's promises are reliable? Why or why not?**

SAY **Now let's learn more about the Great Flood.**

Teacher Skillbuilder

Strive to always keep your promises to your students, no matter how minor the promises may seem. Make sure that this also includes following through, compassionately, on any "promises" of disciplinary action. Students really notice how faithful you are to the promises you make, and the consistency you model will encourage them to become more faithful themselves.

The Ark of God's Mercy

Tell your students that God had to make a choice that was similar to the choices they made in the opening activity, but on a much larger scale. Ask them to think about how God's decision was similar to their choices and how it was different as they listen to the description of what happened in **Genesis 7:1-24.**

SAY **As I read this passage, try to imagine what it must have been like to be one of the members of Noah's family. What would you feel as animals of every size, shape, and color lined up before you? What thoughts would go through your mind as the last of the animals entered the ark and God shut the door? What emotions would you experience as you looked out at your town and friends for the last time? What sounds would you hear as the rain began to pour down? What would the smells inside the ark be like? As the water rose, who or what would you hear on the outside? As the waves began to crash and the boat began to slowly lift off**

For Extra Impact

Show portions of the *Noah's Ark: Fact or Fable?* and the *Noah's Ark: Was There a Worldwide Flood?* videos (available from Group Publishing) for a different perspective on the Great Flood.

Historical Context | Genesis 7:1–8:22; 9:8–16

Genesis 6 wraps up with Noah obeying "God" *(Elohim)*. Chapter 7 begins with "the Lord" *(Yahweh)* speaking to Noah. The use of these two names in these places is noteworthy. The name *Elohim* tends to be used to emphasize God's justice, and the name *Yahweh* most often denotes God's mercy. In chapter 6, Noah carried out God's orders that would result in judgment on humankind. In chapter 7, we see the administration of God's mercy in the salvation of Noah's family and the animals.

Imagine the puzzlement of Noah's neighbors as hundreds of pairs of creatures began wandering toward the ark. No doubt they saw animals they'd never seen before. And then they saw animals they knew and feared walk tamely into the ark. Surely they must have wondered, "Could this Noah guy be right after all?" But we don't read about any of them repenting. They were so hardened in their opposition to the things of God that they couldn't see the truth when it stared them in the face.

When the flood came, it wasn't caused only by rain. We read also that "the springs of the great deep burst forth." Water came shooting upward from under the earth's surface as rain deluged the earth from above. There was so much water that it covered the highest mountains by more than twenty feet! Some scientists believe that this event involved the sliding of continents and the creation of mountain ranges as subterranean plates slid and crashed together. It was likely a very scary time for those inside the ark.

Once the rain stopped, it took almost a year for the water to recede sufficiently for Noah and his family to leave the ark. It's interesting that one of the birds that Noah sent out to see if the earth was getting dry returned with an olive leaf. The olive branch has come to symbolize peace. Perhaps in the time of Noah it symbolized a new peace between God and his creation.

Notice that Noah had a method for testing to see if the earth was dry, but God told him when it was dry (Genesis 8:15). God was taking care of Noah and his family, just as he had promised. When Noah and his family came out of the ark, no one had to tell Noah to worship God. Noah knew that God had done what he had promised in saving them through the ark, and Noah was grateful.

In Genesis 9:12-16, God again demonstrated his love for Noah. God made another promise, signified by the rainbow. The rainbow will always remind us of God's promise to Noah and the fact that God always keeps his promises!

Tip From the Trenches

Practice reading this passage aloud several times before class. Make a note of words you want to emphasize and places you would like to pause or change your volume or pace to help make the passage come alive for your students.

the ground, what would your reaction be? How would you pass the hours and days while you waited for the rain to stop? Close your eyes and picture it as it happens.

Read **Genesis 7:1-24** aloud. As you read, spray teenagers with water and bang cookie sheets together for sound effects at appropriate times.

When you're finished with this section,

ASK
- **What have members of Noah's family experienced so far?**
- **What emotions, thoughts, or sensations stood out to you while you were listening? Explain.**

Ask students to close their eyes again and put themselves back on the ark as you continue to read.

Read **Genesis 8:1-22** aloud. As you read, turn on a fan to blow on students.

ASK • In what ways did this part of the trip feel different from the first part?

• What stood out during this part of the story? Explain.

• What does this story tell you about the reliability of God's promises? Explain.

Bible Application

God's Promises

Have your students get back into their groups from the opening activity, and give each group pens and paper.

SAY **I'd like each group to write and prepare to act out a parable that answers this question:**

• How reliable are God's promises?

SAY **Think about Noah's story as you create your parable, and remember that a parable is a short story that makes a point. You have ten minutes to prepare to present your parable. Each group should conclude its presentation by stating the point of its parable.**

When ten minutes are up, allow each group to perform its parable and state the point.

SAY **The story of the flood is a combination of terror and triumph, a mixture of tragedy and salvation, and a contrast of judgment and mercy.**

ASK • What questions does the story make you ask about God?

• Do you think it would be better if God followed through only on his promises that save people? Why or why not?

• Why do you think it's important that God follows through with what he says he will do?

• Do you think God's promises are reliable? Why or why not?

A God of Justice and Grace

SAY **Let's see what other insight the Bible gives us about judgment, mercy, and God's promises.**

Tip From the Trenches

This passage can raise some very fundamental and emotionally charged questions about God. As a teacher, you'll need to be prepared to listen and empathize with the questions and emotions your students experience. Sometime during the reading or discussion of this story, your students may question how a loving God can destroy a world full of people. Let them know that this is one of the hardest questions for humans to understand, and it's a question that must be wrestled with. Ultimately, your students need to understand that while God is loving, he is also righteous and just. As a holy God, he will not allow sin to go unpunished and to destroy the human race completely. For more explanation of the utter sinfulness of the people of the earth during Noah's day, you may want to consult a Bible commentary. Books such as *The Problem of Pain* by C. S. Lewis can also provide helpful background study to help you prepare for this study.

Give each student a Bible and have him or her follow along as a volunteer reads **Psalm 145:13b**.

ASK **• According to this verse, what has God promised?**

• If God didn't judge his children, what would that say about sin? What would it say about God?

Give each student a pen and a "Hanging in the Balance" handout (p. 64).

SAY **For the people in Noah's day, the water represented God's righteous judgment, but the ark represented God's mercy. Noah responded with a sacrifice of praise and thanksgiving.**

The scale on this handout represents the weight God's promises have in our lives today.

Have students write their names on the side of the scale that represents God's righteous judgment.

SAY **But the cross represents God's mercy through the sacrifice of Jesus Christ.**

Now have students cross out their names and put the name "Jesus" in their places. Have them write their names on the side of the scale that represents mercy.

SAY **It's great to know that a just and powerful God keeps his promises to us in a loving and merciful way.**

Allow a few minutes for your students to write their own responses to this promise-keeping God.

Then invite students to respond in a prayer of praise to God by reading today's Key Verse in unison. Close the prayer by thanking God for his offer of forgiveness and grace to each student that accepts it.

Faith Journal

Give students each an index card and a pen. Have teenagers write their names and answers to the following question on their index cards:

• How has God proved the reliability of his promises to you?

Have teenagers return their index cards to you. Before you meet with the group again, take some time to write personal responses to your students on their index cards. You may want to keep a notebook or a box containing copies of these index cards.

For more information about the Faith Journal option, refer to page 5 in the Introduction.

Tip From the Trenches

To help strengthen the connection between church and home, photocopy the "Taking It Home" page at the end of this study, and either distribute copies to students before they leave or mail them home. Encourage students to complete the reading, activities, and discussion with their families during the coming week.

Music Connection

Give each student an index card and a pen, and have students each write one of God's promises that has proved to be reliable for him or her personally. Pick up the index cards, and redistribute them at random. Have each person read the promise written on his or her index card. Then have each person say a quick prayer of thanks for the reliable promise written on the card he or she is holding.

track 6:
Play the song "Never Forsaken." Have students close their eyes and listen for God's promise in the song. After the song,

ASK
- **What promise did you hear in this song?**
- **How do you think this promise relates to the promises you wrote on your index cards?**
- **How do you think the promise in the song related to Noah and his family in the story?**
- **How can the promise in the song help you as you go through difficult times in your life?**

Never Forsaken

(recorded by Michael Knott from Alternative Worship)

Never forsaken
Never low for more than a while
Never mistaken by anyone else but your child
Never left alone
Never left alone
Never denied forgiveness
Never pushed away
Never far from the goodness
That falls from your path's way
Never left alone
Never left alone
Never left alone
Never left alone
Never forsaken
Never forsaken
Never forsaken
Never forsaken
Never forsaken

promises

[music]

Hanging In the Balance

idea: promises

[t h i n k]

Write a response to God, expressing how it makes you feel to know that he keeps his promises. This could be in the form of a letter, a poem, or a short story.

in the balance

Driving Home the Point:

"A favorite song of mine, 'Seek Ye First,' is based on the words of Matthew 6:33. The lyrics of this song send me a message of hope because they speak to me of God's promise to us: If we make God the center of our lives, seeking God above everything else, we will be blessed.

"This Scripture does not say that God promises us a blue sky every day. Nor does God promise us a smooth path to walk on or a life without sadness or grief. We are promised the strength to make it through rough days and the gift of God's never-ending, never-failing grace and love."

(Devo'Zine, November/December 1996)

keep your word

[take home]

Talking At Home:

Read **Matthew 6:33** together and discuss these questions as a family:

- What does this verse mean to you?
- What has God promised in this verse?
- Do you think this promise is reliable? Why or why not?
- What are some ways you can make the choice to seek God's kingdom first in your own life?

How good are you at keeping your promises? Ask your family to try this experiment:

1. Each family member needs ten pennies.
2. Put a clean glass jar someplace where everyone can find it (such as on the kitchen table, or maybe on top of the TV).
3. Each time someone is "busted" breaking a promise, that person will be cordially invited to donate one penny to the jar.
4. After a week, count the pennies in the jar. How might things have been different if everyone had kept all of their promises (and all of their pennies)? Why is it important for God to be a promise-keeper?

Read and think about **Numbers 23:19**.

Sky-High Rebellion

Genesis 11:1-9

7

People Build a Tower at Babel

 **key question:** How should we feel about God?

 **study focus:** Students will learn that God's way is the best way.

Key Verse: "Love the Lord your God with all your heart and with all your soul and with all your strength." Deuteronomy 6:5

A Look at the Study

Study Sequence	Minutes	What Students Will Do	Classroom Supplies
Getting Started	5 to 10	**The Story of Humanity**—Create an ongoing story and compare it to the ongoing story of human sin and rebellion in the book of Genesis.	
	5 to 10	**Attitude Charades**—Discover that we can often communicate what we're feeling without saying a word.	Slips of paper; pens; a hat, box, or basket
Bible Story Exploration	5 to 10	**Tower of Disobedience**—Explore background information about the Tower of Babel.	Newsprint, tape, markers, "Historical Context" copies (p. 71), pen
	15 to 20	**My Way or the Highway**—Examine the story of the Tower of Babel and compare God's commands to the people's responses throughout the book of Genesis.	Bibles, "My Way or the Highway" handouts (p. 75), pens
Bible Application	5 to 10	**The Domino Effect**—Attempt to build a domino tower and then commit their attitudes and actions to God.	Bible, dominoes
	up to 5	**Faith Journal**—Explore the Key Question and respond in writing.	Index cards, pens
Music Connection	5 to 10	**Store**—Explore "treasures" they're storing for themselves on earth. Use this option at an appropriate time in the study.	Bible, paper, pens, CD: "Store" (Track 7), CD player

Age-Level Insight

Adolescents often think they're immortal. They may believe that things which threaten the well-being of others cannot touch them. Consequently, they may not think they need God or anyone else; they consider themselves "invincible." Draw teenagers' attention to the needs they've had in the past and how God has met those needs. Patiently help them discover that God provides the place where they can spread their wings.

Last Week's Impact

As teenagers arrive, greet them warmly and ask follow-up questions to review last week's study and Key Verse. Ask questions such as "What did you learn about God's promises?" and "What did you discover about your family's ability to keep promises?"

If you used the Faith Journal option last week, take this time to return your students' index cards to them.

Getting Started

The Story of Humanity

Have students form a circle.

SAY **I'd like us to create a story together. This story will be about what last week was like for each of us. Think of something unusual, funny, or interesting that happened to you last week. I'll start the story by sharing one sentence about something that happened to me. Then the person next to me will continue the story by adding something that happened to him or her. For example, I might start the story by saying, "Last week, I went to the circus for the first time." The next person might continue the story by saying, "I flew to Hawaii and back." We'll continue around the circle with each person adding to the story. The last person in the circle will conclude the story.**

Begin the story by sharing your sentence, and then have students continue the story around the circle. When the story is finished,

SAY **Just as we got to watch our own story unfold, we've also been able to watch an ongoing story unfold in our study in the book of Genesis during the past six weeks.**

ASK
- **What do the stories about Adam and Eve, Cain and Abel, and Noah and the people of the world have in common?**
- **What type of progression can you see from one story to the next?**
- **Why do you think each generation failed to learn from the previous ones in spite of terrible consequences?**

- **How do you think God's people felt about God in these stories?**

For Extra Impact

To add to the atmosphere and pressure, bring a kitchen timer and set it for one minute so students can hear the seconds ticking away before the bell rings.

Attitude Charades

SAY **The progression of sinful action in spite of terrible consequences continues in the next story. In this story, the people demonstrated their attitudes toward God through their actions. Often we can demonstrate our attitudes toward those around us without saying a word. We're about to play a game that demonstrates the ability to silently communicate negative attitudes.**

Write the following attitude words on slips of paper: hate, rebellion, pride, self-centeredness, jealousy, and sin. Have students form two teams.

SAY **Now I'd like you to play a quick game of Attitude Charades.**

One or two at a time, the members of your team will draw an attitude word out of this hat [or box or basket] **and then act out the word for the rest of the team to guess. The actors will have thirty seconds to act out the word. If the rest of the team guesses the word, that team gets a point. You'll need to make sure that everyone on your team gets a chance to act; this might mean that several people will create a pantomime together to act out one of the words.**

Designate a team to go first, and keep time while teams are acting.

ASK

- **Did you find it difficult or easy to get others to understand the attitude you were communicating? Why?**
- **Do you think other people know when you're upset with them even when you don't tell them about it?**
- **What are some ways other people can know the way you're feeling?**
- **How does God know the way you're feeling?**

- **What should our attitude be toward God?**
- **How can we demonstrate this attitude?**

SAY **Many times, we feel justified when we have a bad attitude toward another person. But how should we feel about a perfect, all-powerful God? In the story we are about to read, the people chose to shake their fists in the face of God in defiance of him.**

for OLDER teenagers

To create a more reflective activity for older teenagers, provide materials such as poster board or newsprint, markers, old magazines, scissors, tape, and glue, and have them each create a storyboard about one of the attitude words. Have them each detail what the attitude may "look" like and feel like, ways the attitude might be expressed both verbally and nonverbally, a narrative example of the attitude from their own lives, and where they think the attitude stems from. When they're finished creating, have teenagers share their attitude boards with the whole group. Continue the activity with the debriefing questions at the end.

Bible Story Exploration

Tower of Disobedience

Hang a sheet of newsprint on the wall, and divide the sheet into two columns. Label one column "What We Know Already" and the other column "Questions We Still Have."

SAY **I'd like you to begin your study of the story of the Tower of Babel by gathering and studying some background information. The first step in this process is to discover what we already know about this story.**

Have students call out details or facts about the story they already know, and write them on the newsprint.

SAY **Now I'd like you to think of anything we don't know about this story. What questions do you have?**

Tip From the Trenches

The "Historical Context" box may not answer all students' questions. If this happens, encourage students to seek answers as they read the Bible story itself or to research the questions in Bible commentaries or other resources.

Have students call out any questions they may have about the story, and write the questions on the newsprint. Then give each student a copy of the "Historical Context" box (p. 71) and a pen.

SAY **I'd like each of you to read this information about the Tower of Babel. As you read, underline answers to the questions we asked. When you're finished, turn the paper over and write any interesting or unusual facts you discovered from your reading.**

Give students a few minutes to read and respond, and then have them get back into their teams from the previous activity. Have them share the information they gathered with their team members. Then have each team select two or three things to share with the class, and have one person from each team share.

ASK
- **What does this information tell you about God?**
- **What does the information tell you about humans?**

- **According to your research, how do you think we should feel about God?**

SAY **Let's learn more about how the people in this story felt about God.**

My Way or the Highway

Make sure each student has a Bible, and ask a volunteer to read **Genesis 11:1-9** aloud.

SAY **While the passage is being read, I'd like the rest of you to listen and follow along in your Bibles. Try to detect the sinful attitudes the human race added to its ongoing list of sins against its Creator. To get started, think of the attitudes you acted out a few minutes ago. When you hear a sinful attitude displayed, I'd like you to call out, "Sinful attitude!"**

When the volunteer has finished reading, ask your students to share the sinful attitudes they heard in the story. Then have students form pairs.

SAY **Now I'd like you to work together to discover how the people in this passage responded to God.**

Give each pair a "My Way or the Highway" handout (p. 75) and a pen, and have the pairs use their Bibles to complete the handout.

After pairs have completed the handouts, have students come back together as a large group. Go through the questions on the handout one at a time, allowing volunteers to share their answers.

Historical Context | Genesis 11:1-9

The pattern continues. Just a few generations and only 150 to 200 years after the miraculous saving of Noah's family in the ark, the descendants of those ark-dwellers turned away from God. After Noah came out of the ark, one of God's commands to him was to "fill the earth." It appears that God wanted people to spread out across the earth, but some of the people decided to group together in a city, make a name for themselves, and keep themselves from being scattered. They showed no concern for glorifying or obeying God. And Noah lived to see all of this happen, as Genesis 9:28 tells us that Noah lived 350 years after the flood!

The people's intent in building a tower was not to reach heaven, as some have suggested. They wanted to build something showy that would bring them recognition. People from all around would see the tall tower that seemed to reach into the heavens. Others would marvel at what they had done, and they would be proud. These people weren't interested in serving God; rather they wanted to elevate their own standing before others. In essence, they tried to make themselves look more important than God.

God's response again appears to be one of sorrow. If these people were able to do such a self-serving, God-defying thing as to build this tower, what other evil things were next on the horizon? Who would stop the decline? How long would it be before none were left who honored God? God wanted people to depend on him, and instead they were trying to compete with him. So again, more out of concern for keeping people from further evil than out of a desire to punish, God put a stop to what was happening by causing people to speak different languages.

It's interesting to think about how God might have used this incident to differentiate various races. By selectively giving certain individuals the same language, God could have directed which people clustered together, and their gene pools could have resulted in races with very different physical characteristics, such as exist today. Whatever happened, the people were scattered, just as God intended.

Some ancient reports indicate that an unfinished tower stood—perhaps for centuries—just outside of the city of Babylon. Isn't it just like God to take something that evil people intended as a monument to themselves and turn it into a monument to his power and sovereignty? God wants us all to remember what he's done for us and how much we need him!

After each question,

ASK • **What did you learn about God from this passage?**

• **What did you learn about the nature of the human race?**

• **What did you learn about God's relationship with the human race?**

After the group has finished going through the handout,

ASK • **Why do you think people choose to rebel against God?**

• **In what ways are people today like the people in Genesis 11? In what ways are they different?**

• **How do you think God wants people to feel about him?**

Bible Application

The Domino Effect

Scatter a set of dominoes on a table.

SAY **Now we're going to see how high you can build a domino tower.**

Have teenagers follow these rules:

- The dominoes must be stacked by standing them up on one end, not by laying them flat.
- Each person will take a turn adding a domino to the tower.
- If the tower falls over, the group must begin building again with the next person.

Allow students to continue trying to build a tower until it has fallen down several times. Then stop the building and collect the dominoes.

ASK
- **How did you feel during this exercise? Do you think it was a success or a failure?**
- **How is this like what we sometimes do in our own lives?**

SAY **You may have had some success in building a tower, and you may even have built it higher than you thought possible. However, ultimately your efforts were a failure; sooner or later, the tower fell down.**

Like the people in Genesis 11, we often attempt to live our lives our way and ignore God. We think we know what is best for our own lives. This attitude may work for a while, but sooner or later it will end in failure.

SAY **Now I'd like each of you to take a domino and hold it in your hand. Then close your eyes, and silently ask God to show you an area of your life in which your attitudes or actions ignore God and what he wants for you. Let the domino you're holding represent that attitude or action.**

Give students a few moments to think and pray silently, and then read **Deuteronomy 6:5** aloud.

SAY **Now, if you're willing to turn that area of your life over to God and live the life he wants you to live, I'd like you to place your domino on the table and personalize Deuteronomy 6:5 by saying, "I choose to love the Lord my God with all my heart and with all my soul and with all my strength."**

Give students a few moments to do this, and then close the activity with a prayer of dedication on behalf of your students.

Tip From the Trenches

If you have a large group, you may want to divide students into several groups and use more than one set of dominoes.

Tip From the Trenches

If you don't have access to dominoes, use pennies or playing cards instead.

For Extra Impact

Have students form a cross with their dominoes when they're finished.

for Younger teenagers

To help younger teenagers get into a more reflective mood, you may want to play soothing, quiet music in the background and have them sit apart from each other. Also, it might help to have them write down their responses.

Faith Journal

Give students each an index card and a pen. Have teenagers write their names and answers to the following question on their index cards:

• How can you use your attitudes and actions to glorify God?

Have teenagers return their index cards to you. Before you meet with the group again, take some time to write personal responses to your students on their index cards. You may want to keep a notebook or a box containing copies of these index cards.

For more information about the Faith Journal option, refer to page 5 in the Introduction.

Tip From the Trenches

To help strengthen the connection between church and home, photocopy the "Taking It Home" page at the end of this study, and either distribute copies to students before they leave or mail them home. Encourage students to complete the reading, activities, and discussion with their families during the coming week.

Music Connection

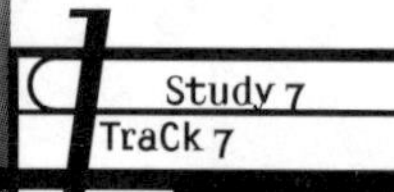

idea:listen

possessions

Give students each four slips of paper and a pen, and have them write one "treasure" on each slip of paper.

track 7:

Read **Matthew 6:19-21** aloud, and then play the song "Store." As the song is playing, have students think about ways that people "store" treasure for themselves on earth. After each verse, pause the CD, and have students choose two of their treasures to give up and share them with the group. After the song,

ASK

- **What are some treasures that people store for themselves on earth?**
- **Why is this wrong? Where should people store their treasures?**
- **What does it mean to store treasures in heaven?**
- **How did the people in the Bible story try to store treasure on earth?**
- **What should they have done differently?**

Store

(recorded by According to John)

I like toys just as much as the next guy—
Cellular noise reachin' out to touch someone.
But I don't rely on the creature comforts.
I'll tell you why, I'll tell you why—they don't offer peace of mind.
'Cause like grass and flowered fields
All this will blow away.

Chorus:
Don't store any more treasure for yourself
Where moth and rust destroy,
And the thief breaks down the door—steals your toys.
Don't store any more (more).
Don't you know (don't you know) there's a better life (a better life)?
So don't store any more treasure in this world;
Store it above the sky.

Above the sky, there's a place prepared for you;
Above the sky, the Creator's counting days (hey, yeah).
So why cling to what you cannot hold—
Why miss the golden streets for fool's gold?
'Cause like grass and flowered fields
All this will blow away.

Chorus:
Don't store any more treasure for yourself
Where moth and rust destroy,
And the thief breaks down the door—steals your toys.
Don't store any more (more)—
Don't you know (don't you know) there's another life (another life)?
So don't store any more treasure in this world;
Store it above the sky.

'Cause like grass and flowered fields
All this will blow away (blow away).

Chorus:
Don't store any more treasure for yourself
Where moth and rust destroy,
And the thief breaks down the door—steals your toys.
Don't store any more (more).

Repeat Chorus:

No, no—
Don't store,
Don't store,
Don't store any more,
Don't store any more.
Hey!

My Way or the Highway

Study 7 ....

idea:expectations

From the beginning of Genesis, God laid out certain expectations that he had for the people of the earth. Use your Bible to compare God's expectations with the attitudes or actions of his people.

1. Compare what God commanded the human race to do in **Genesis 1:28** and **Genesis 9:7** with what the people decided to do in **Genesis 11:2** and **Genesis 11:4**.

2. Compare what the people were doing that grieved God in **Genesis 6:5** with what the people were trying to do again in **Genesis 11:6**.

3. Compare the attitude Noah had toward his Creator in Genesis 8:20 with the attitude the people had toward their Creator in **Genesis 11:4**.

4. Compare the power God used to punish a rebellious and sinful people in **Genesis 7:17-21** with the attitude the people had about their own power in **Genesis 11:3-4**.

5. How should God's people have felt about God? What should they have done to express the way they felt?

6. How did the people feel about God? What did they do to express the way they felt?

[think]

following

Taking It Home

idea:discuss Talking About It

Driving Home the Point:

"When I was younger, I thought that asking God into my heart once was enough to set me on the right path forever. I figured that because I'd been baptized and confirmed into my church, God was automatically the center of my life. I couldn't figure out why I still felt so far from him so much of the time.

"I told a wise friend about my problem, and I asked her why it felt like God was so far away. 'I asked him into my heart,' I said. 'Doesn't he care about me?'

" 'Did you ask him into your heart this morning?' she asked.

" 'Well... no.'

" 'How about yesterday?'

" 'Umm... I guess not.'

"She went on to explain that even after we become Christians, we have to continue to ask God to be a part of our lives, each and every day. He wants to be in constant communication with us, and communication is definitely a two-way street." (1998-1999 Student Plan-It Calendar)

[take home]

every day

Talking At Home:

Read **Deuteronomy 6:6-7** together and answer these questions honestly (either silently or out loud):

- Did I ask God into my heart today?
- How is my relationship with God?
- Does anything in my life seem to be "in the way" of a closer relationship with God?
- What can I do to become closer to God?

Think of God as the "unseen guest" that lives in your home. Include him in your family life by noticing and acknowledging his involvement in some aspect of your life at least once a day. (Where's God when you're doing your homework?) As you make a conscious effort to think and speak about God, it will help you remember your commitment to put him first in your heart and life.

Faith: A Pilgrim's Process

Genesis 12:1-8

8

Abram Follows God's Direction

key question: Why should we trust God?

study focus: Students will be prompted to think about times God was directing them, even though they might not have known where they were going.

key verse: "Trust in the Lord with all your heart and lean not on your own understanding; in all your ways acknowledge him, and he will make your paths straight." Proverbs 3:5-6

A Look at the Study

Study Sequence	Minutes	What Students Will Do	Classroom Supplies
Getting Started	15 to 20	**Heroes of the Faith**—Research the lives of various heroes of the faith and introduce them to the group.	Resource books, "Heroes of the Faith" handouts (p. 85), pens
Bible Story Exploration	5 to 10	**Abram's Journey**—Explore background information about Abram's journey.	Bibles, "Historical Context" copies (p. 80), pens, poster board or newsprint, markers
	10 to 15	**Trusting God's Promises**— Discuss the story of Abram's call and then write journal entries from the main characters' points of view.	Bible, paper, pens
Bible Application	15 to 20	**Leap of Faith**—Illustrate their own "leaps of faith" and then share them with the group.	Bibles; grocery bag containing art supplies such as crayons or markers, scissors, construction paper, tape, glue, stapler, stickers, and old magazines; poster board; newsprint; tape; markers
	up to 5	**Faith Journal**—Explore the Key Question and respond in writing.	Index cards, pens
Music Connection	5 to 10	**Watershed**—Explore ways God might comfort and strengthen them during times of confusion. Use this option at an appropriate time in the study.	Paper, pens, CD: "Watershed" (Track 8), CD player

Age-Level Insight

Teenagers trust their peers and people they believe to be "cool." Parents, teachers, and other adults are suspect unless they have worked hard to earn a teenager's respect. If teenagers view God as someone with a set of rules made only to spoil their fun, they're not going to trust God. But if a foundation of truth about God's character was laid earlier in teenagers' lives, they may question some things about God and experiment with different identities, but, ultimately, they will trust God. Be consistent and trustworthy with the teenagers you teach. You will earn their respect and trust and help them understand and believe in God's trustworthiness.

Last Week's Impact

As teenagers arrive, greet them warmly and ask follow-up questions to review last week's study and Key Verse. Ask questions such as "What attitudes and actions does the human race often show toward God?" and "How can you grow closer to God?"

If you used the Faith Journal option last week, take this time to return your students' index cards to them.

Heroes of the Faith Resources

(Note: This is not a comprehensive list; ask your pastor or a librarian for additional resources.)

Scientists Who Believe: 21 Tell Their Own Stories by Eric C. Barrett and David Fisher
70 Great Christians by G. Hanks
They Walked in the Spirit by Douglas M. Strong
Living With the Giants: The Lives of Great Men of the Faith by Warren W. Wiersbe
Victorious Christians You Should Know by Warren W. Wiersbe

Tip From the Trenches

If it is difficult or impossible to obtain resource books for this activity, have students identify their own heroes instead.

Getting Started

Heroes of the Faith

Begin the study by telling students that you're going to be talking today about trusting God.

ASK

- **Why should God be trusted?**

SAY **To find the answer to that question, we're going to start by taking a look at some "heroes of the faith"—people who put their trust in God.**

Divide the class into five groups, and assign each group the name of a person found in the kinds of books listed in the "Heroes of the Faith Resources" box in the margin. (Don't assign Abram to a group, as the class will discuss his life later in the study.) Give each group a "Heroes of the Faith" handout (p. 85) and pens, and tell groups you want them to discuss what they know about their assigned people using knowledge they have already and information in the book or books you've provided. Each group should then discuss the questions on the handout and be prepared to "introduce" its person to the class.

After ten or fifteen minutes, have each group introduce its person to the rest of the class.

Bible Story Exploration

Abram's Journey

Lay out the supplies, and give each student a copy of the "Historical Context" box (p. 80), a Bible, and a pen.

SAY **I'd like you to begin your study of Abram's journey by studying some background information. I'll assign each group a topic and a presentation format. For example, one group will be the Drama group, one group will be the Song group, and so on. As you read the information I've given you, I'd like you to be thinking about the topic and the presentation format I've assigned you. When you're finished reading, I'd like you to create a brief presentation that tells about your assigned topic.**

Assign groups the following topics and presentation formats (it's OK if more than one group has the same topic and format):

- Abram's relationship with God (Song)

• Abram's journey (Drama)

• Lot's participation (Poster)

Invite students to take their research further by including information from the Bible story.

Give groups a few minutes to read the information and create their presentations, and then have them make the presentations to the whole class.

ASK • **What does this information tell you about God?**

• **Based on your research, why do you think we should trust God?**

SAY **Let's learn more about Abram's journey.**

Trusting God's Promises

Give each student a piece of paper and a pen.

SAY **Now let's hear what the Bible has to say about Abram, a man who had to decide whether to trust God. As I read these verses aloud, jot down as many details as you can about Abram. Then I'll follow up with some questions.**

Read **Genesis 12:1-8** aloud, pausing between verses.

ASK • **What facts do we know about Abram from this text?**

• **Assuming he believed God, what did Abram know for sure when he left his home?**

• **What did Abram do after God made his promise?**

• **What reasons might Abram have had for trusting God?**

SAY **Only when Abram had traveled all the way to Shechem did God tell him that the land of Canaan would eventually belong to Abram's descendants.**

ASK • **If you had been in Abram's shoes and knew that Canaan was already inhabited, how do you think you might have reacted to this promise?**

• **Why do you think God made his promise at Shechem (rather than earlier)? Why do you think Abram built an altar at Shechem?**

• **Considering the fact that "the locals" worshipped many different gods, how do you think they might have reacted to Abram's altars?**

Have students return to their groups from the previous activity.

Teacher Skillbuilder

We can learn much by noting the nuances of Jesus' teaching style. For example, Jesus had a way of quietly getting his audience's attention. One example is the time he defused a potentially violent situation by stooping to write in the dust **(John 8:8)**. If you want to pique your students' curiosity, do something unexpected: After they have arrived, enter the room silently, write "Follow me" on the board, and then walk out the door. Go to a new location—even if it's just the hallway—to begin the study.

Next, sit down on the floor. The Gospels record that Jesus made a habit of getting right in the midst of the people he was teaching.

Finally, Jesus often addressed people by name, making each individual feel special. Do this frequently during studies to help teenagers feel that the information you're sharing pertains to each one of them.

For Extra Impact

To help students identify a bit more with Abram's total trust in God, have students try trust falls into each other's arms. Be sure to have spotters to keep anyone from getting hurt.

Historical Context | Genesis 12: 1-8

"Sell everything you can't carry with you, leave all your friends and extended family, get your wife and belongings in the car, and start driving. You'll probably never come back here again, but don't worry about that—I'll show you where to go." If God were speaking to Abram today, that might be what he'd say. What trust in God it took for Abram to leave his home, his country, and everything familiar and comfortable and set out for an unknown destination, having only God's command to go on!

Abram had not only the concerns of leaving the familiar behind, but also the worries of keeping the things he took with him. Abram was apparently a wealthy man, with a lot of sheep, cattle, and other livestock. In those days, traveling with herds in unknown territory was treacherous. Besides, Abram was seventy-five years old! How could he know they'd be safe for even the first week of the months-long journey God led them on? He might have questioned if he'd even be alive the next day! But he trusted and followed God.

What helped Abram on his way was a trusting relationship with God and the promises of blessing that would benefit not only his household but "all the peoples on earth"! Even though those promises might have been hard to believe, they were all Abram needed.

Lot, Abram's nephew, went along but probably not just for companionship or adventure. It was a disgrace in that culture to not have descendants, and Abram realized that he and his wife were getting too old to have children. Abram may have asked Lot to go because Abram had no offspring of his own to take charge if Abram died or became incapacitated. Or Lot may have seen this as an opportunity to inherit Abram's riches, knowing that his uncle was bound to die before long. Either way, Lot probably was expected to be Abram's heir.

We are told nothing about the journey, but the trip from Haran to Bethel was approximately five hundred miles, much of it over rough desert land. Water for all of Abram's flocks and entourage would have been a constant concern, and they probably took only food with them. Conflict with local residents was likely a daily occurrence, and the trip probably took several months.

Finally Abram completed the journey in faith, and now, in Genesis 12:7, the Lord appeared to him. God had spoken to Abram earlier, but now God appeared and confirmed the promise he had made to Abram back at Haran: The fertile land before him would one day belong to his descendants. That meant he would still have descendants! The promises were beginning to come true!

Abram built an altar to honor God through worship. "Calling upon the name of the Lord" meant worshipping him and acknowledging him as God. Abram knew that God had blessed him already and that many more blessings were still to come. Abram's trust in God was beginning to pay off!

for Younger teenagers

Instead of writing journal entries, younger teenagers might enjoy creating role-plays or skits that explore the attitudes and emotions of the main characters of this story.

SAY **To experience this story a little further, I'd like you to think about the passage, the notes you jotted down about Abram, and the discussion we just had. Then I'd like each group to write a journal entry that might have been written by Abram, Lot, or Sarai during the time that Abram was called. Include possible feelings, attitudes, and thoughts of your group's chosen character. Write your journal entry on the back of one of your pieces of paper.**

Give groups a few minutes to do this, and then have them share their journal entries with the larger group.

SAY **As we can see, Abram put a lot of trust in God. Now let's explore ways that we can put our trust in God.**

Bible Application

Leap of Faith

Have teenagers form a circle. Dump the contents of the grocery bag onto the floor in the center of the circle, and give each student a piece of poster board. Challenge students each to think about a time in their life when they took a leap of faith—when their belief or trust in something (or someone) resulted in some kind of action. For example, one student might illustrate a time he tried out for a sport even though the odds of making the team weren't great. Another student might recall visiting an AIDS patient despite feeling uneasy about it, while someone else might remember initiating a conversation at the risk of being rejected. Ask each student to use the art supplies you've provided to create a storyboard illustrating that event or situation. Write the following questions on newsprint, and tape the newsprint to a wall. Have students divide their storyboards into five panels, one for each question.

- Where were you when you started this particular faith journey?
- What did you leave behind?
- What did you take with you?
- What were the "Canaanites," or obstacles, that you encountered along the way?
- Where did you end up?

Ask teenagers to incorporate the answers to the questions in their illustrations.

Give teenagers about five minutes to create their storyboards, and then have students pair up and explain their creations to their partners.

Give pairs a few minutes to share.

SAY **Now I want you to look at your own storyboards again and reflect silently on the following questions.**

ASK

- **What prompted you to begin your journey?**
- **When you started this journey, did you know where you would end up?**
- **Who or what did you put your faith in?**
- **If you were trusting God to lead you, did you have a "Shechem"—a place where you showed your allegiance to him? If so, was your "altar" visible to other people?**

SAY **We know that we should trust God, but for most of us, faith is a process, a journey during which we have periods of confidence and moments of doubt. Now I want you to think about the questions I'm going to ask you, but this time I'd like you to share your answers with the class.**

ASK
- **When do you feel most convinced of God's love and concern for you?**
- **What kinds of circumstances cause you to doubt God?**
- **What purpose might God have in mind for you?**

- **Why should you trust God?**

SAY **The lives of faithful people such as the ones we've discussed today show us that we can trust God, no matter what situations we find ourselves in, because he has a plan for our lives. Just like these heroes of faith, we can live with the assurance that God is always with us, showing us where to go.**

Have students open their Bibles to Proverbs, and read **Proverbs 3:5-6** aloud.

SAY **I'd like you to take a few moments to prayerfully reflect on the many reasons God gives you to trust in him. Then we'll pray a prayer of commitment together by paraphrasing and personalizing these verses from Proverbs.**

End the study by having students pray in unison: **I will trust in the Lord with all my heart and lean not on my own understanding; in all my ways I will acknowledge him, and he will make my paths straight.**

Faith Journal

Give students each an index card and a pen. Have teenagers write their names and answers to the following question on their index cards:

- How can your trust in God be strengthened?

Have teenagers return their index cards to you. Before you meet with the group again, take some time to write personal responses to your students on their index cards. You may want to keep a notebook or a box containing copies of these index cards.

For more information about the Faith Journal option, refer to page 5 in the Introduction.

The Way It Was

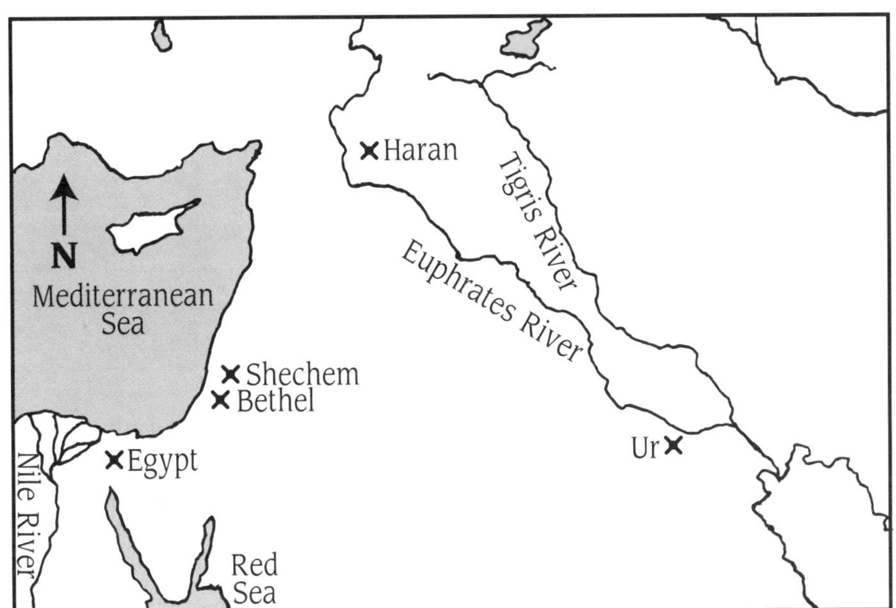

For Extra Impact

Help students visualize Abram's journey by creating a map. Use the map provided in "The Way It Was" box at left to chart Abram's journey on a long piece of newsprint. Draw a rough sketch of the region referred to in **Genesis 12:1-8,** labeling key landmarks (the Mediterranean Sea, the Red Sea, Egypt, the cities of Ur and Haran, the altar locations at Shechem and Bethel, the Euphrates River, the Tigris River, and the Nile River). Hang this map somewhere in the room.

Invite students to illustrate Abram's journey using the art supplies provided for the "Leap of Faith" activity. Leave the map up for students to embellish during today's study or in the weeks ahead as they continue their study of Genesis.

Tip From the Trenches

To help strengthen the connection between church and home, photocopy the "Taking It Home" page at the end of this study, and either distribute copies to students before they leave or mail them home. Encourage students to complete the reading, activities, and discussion with their families during the coming week.

[mu/Sic]

Music Connection

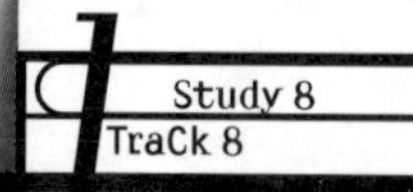

idea:listen

Give students paper and pens.

track 8:
Play the song "Watershed." As the song is playing, have students close their eyes and listen for words or phrases they would find comforting and strengthening in their faith journeys. After the song,

ASK
- **What are some of the words and phrases you heard?**
- **How do you think those words or phrases would have comforted and strengthened Abram in his journey? How could they comfort and strengthen you?**

Have students form pairs. Have members of each pair identify a person they know (it might be one of them) who is going through a time of confusion or frustration in his or her faith journey. Have pairs write short letters of comfort and strength to those people, using the words and phrases they identified in the song.

Watershed

(recorded by Chaos Is the Poetry)

I am weary, I am tired,
I have failed on feet of fire.
Lord, grant me wisdom; keep me fed;
Guide me through the watershed.

Lead me to the golden meadows;
Lead me to a better place.
Let me hear the words you said;
Lead me through the watershed.

I'm a stranger, far from home—
I'm a liar in flesh and bone.
I'm a child; break thy bread.
Help me through the watershed.

Help me find a place that's safe
Where I can think and I can pray.
In your hands, a spool and thread—
I'll meet you in the watershed.

I am grateful to have known;
I am grateful I'm reborn—
Your spirit's raised me from the dead
Crossing through the watershed.

life is a journey

Heroes of the Faith

Research your assigned person using the resources provided, and answer the following questions about your person.

• Who is the person? What did he or she do?

• What risks did this person have to take in order to achieve what he or she did?

• Was there a point when this person might have felt very alone?

• What positive outcomes resulted from this person's faith?

• Why should this person have trusted God?

Condense the information you've discovered into a brief "introduction" paragraph. You'll be introducing your person to the whole group.

[think]

trust in God

idea:discuss Talking About It

[take home] letting go

Driving Home the Point:

"A man named Jack was walking along a steep cliff one day when he accidentally got too close to the edge and fell. On the way down he grabbed a branch, which temporarily stopped his fall. He looked down and to his horror saw that the canyon fell straight down for more than a thousand feet. He couldn't hang onto the branch forever, and there was no way for him to climb up the steep wall of the cliff.

"So Jack began yelling for help, hoping that someone passing by would hear him and lower a rope or something...He yelled for hours, but no one heard him. He was about to give up when he heard a voice.

" 'Jack. Jack. Can you hear me?'

" 'Yes, yes! I can hear you. I'm down here!'

" 'I can see you, Jack. Are you all right?'

" 'Yes, but... who are you, and where are you?'

" 'I am the Lord, Jack. I'm everywhere.'

" 'The Lord? You mean, God?'

" 'That's me.'

" 'God, please help me! I promise—if you'll get me down from here, I'll stop sinning. I'll be a really good person. I'll serve you for the rest of my life.'

" 'Easy on the promises, Jack. Let's just get you down from there; then we can talk. Now, here's what I want you to do. Listen carefully.'

" 'I'll do anything, Lord. Just tell me what to do.'

" 'OK. Let go of the branch.'

" 'What?'

" 'I said, let go of the branch. Just trust me. Let go.'

"There was a long silence. Finally Jack yelled, 'Help! Help! Is anyone else up there?'"

(**Wayne Rice,** Hot Illustrations for Youth Talks)

Talking At Home:

Read **Matthew 11:29-30** together and discuss these questions:

- Do you sometimes find it difficult to follow the will of God? Explain.
- What promise did Christ give us in the verse? How might this promise help us trust him?

Work with your family to create a storyboard showing Jesus' faith journey, identifying events or circumstances that might have strengthened or shaken his faith, "Canaanites" he encountered along the way, and "Shechems" where he proclaimed his allegiance to God. What did Jesus gain by trusting in God? What did we gain because Jesus trusted in God?

You Go First

Genesis 13:1-18

9

Lot and Abram Divide the Land

 **key question:** How should we treat others?

 **study focus:** Teenagers will learn what the Bible says about the way they should treat other people.

key verse: "Do to others as you would have them do to you." Luke 6:31

A Look at the Study

Study Sequence	Minutes	What Students Will Do	Classroom Supplies
Getting Started	5 to 10	**Doughnut Decisions**—Decide how much of a doughnut to share and then discuss the difficulties of putting others before themselves.	Doughnuts
Bible Story Exploration	10 to 15	**Abram's Sacrifice**—Explore background information about the story of Abram and Lot.	Bibles, "Historical Context" copies (p. 90), poster board or newsprint, old magazines, scissors, glue sticks
	10 to 15	**Whose Sacrifice Is Greater?**—Examine the emotions contained in the story of Abram and Lot and then create their own scenarios using similar emotions.	Bibles, paper plates, markers
	10 to 15	**Givers and Takers**—Explore several Bible passages about people who either give or take.	Bibles, "Givers and Takers" handout (p. 96), pens, newsprint, tape, markers
Bible Application	5 to 10	**I'm Here to Serve**—Serve or be served snacks, based on numbers on their backs.	Doughnuts, napkins, cups, pitchers of juice, masking tape, markers
	5 to 10	**Rating My Ability**—Determine how well they do at putting others first and then commit to putting the other person first in a specific relationship.	Bible, index cards, pens
	up to 5	**Faith Journal**—Explore the Key Question and respond in writing.	Index cards, pens
Music Connection	5 to 10	**Forgive Forget**—Discuss how forgiveness is one way of putting others' needs ahead of their own. Use this option at an appropriate time in the study.	Bibles, CD: "Forgive Forget" (Track 9), CD player

Age-Level Insight

The teenage years can be emotionally volatile. Families can be torn apart because of the squabbling brought about by having teenagers in the house. Same-sex and opposite-sex relationships are experimental and immature and can result in emotional pain and anger. Create a safe place for teenagers to talk about the difficulties they're encountering in relationships of all kinds. Counsel them in their choices of friends and in the storms of family life. Help teenagers to understand God's principles for relationships, and show them concrete ways they can put these principles into practice.

Last Week's Impact

As teenagers arrive, greet them warmly and ask follow-up questions to review last week's study and Key Verse. Ask questions such as "What are some things you can do to help you trust in God more completely?" and "What did your family learn about Jesus' faith journey?"

If you used the Faith Journal option last week, take this time to return your students' index cards to them.

Teacher Skillbuilder

God's message to "do to others as you would have them do to you" stands in contrast to what society has taught teenagers. Putting friends' needs or desires ahead of their own might be quite difficult for some students. Many students struggle with this issue—maybe their parents model an erroneous way of thinking, or maybe someone they put first has burned them. Whatever the issue is, remember that your teenagers might have difficulty with the idea of putting others first.

Getting Started

Doughnut Decisions

Have students form pairs, and have each pair choose one partner to be the leader. Give each leader one doughnut.

SAY **Leaders, you're allowed to eat as much of your doughnuts as you'd like, but you also need to save some doughnut for your partners. Break off as much of the doughnut as you'd like and then eat it. Then give the other portion of the doughnut to your partner.**

ASK the partners:

- **How do you feel about the amount your leader gave you?**
- **Was your leader fair in the amount he or she gave you? Why or why not?**
- **How do you think you would have felt if your leader's division of the doughnut was less fair?**

ASK the leaders:

- **How did you decide how much of the doughnut your partner should get?**

Gather everyone in the center of your meeting room. Ask teenagers to respond to the following statements by standing up if they agree or sitting down if they disagree. For every statement, ask teenagers to share a particular situation in their own lives that fits the statement.

- **I would be disappointed if I got less of something than my friends got.**
- **I have given someone something I didn't like and was finished using.**
- **I have given someone the best I had while I have made do with less.**
- **I think the best way to put others first is by letting them have their own way.**
- **I have a hard time giving away things that I really like.**

ASK the group:

- **Have you ever put someone's needs or desires ahead of yours? When?**
- **How do you feel when you put someone's needs ahead of yours?**

- **What models are we given in today's media and politics for the way we should treat each other?**

• How should we treat each other according to God?

Bible Story Exploration

Abram's Sacrifice

Give each student a copy of the "Historical Context" box (p. 90), a Bible, a piece of poster board or newsprint, some old magazines, scissors, and glue sticks.

SAY **I'd like you to begin your study of the story of Lot and Abram by looking at some background information.**

Have students return to their pairs from the previous activity, and assign each pair one of these characters: Lot or Abram.

SAY **Each pair is going to act as an illustrating team. I'd like you to read the information I've given you. When you're finished reading, I'd like you to answer the following questions about your character that you've found in the information you've read.**

- **Who?**
- **What?**
- **Where?**
- **When?**
- **Why?**
- **How?**

Make sure to include any important information as you answer these questions. Then use the information you've gathered and the material provided to create a montage that you'll share in our classroom "gallery."

Invite students to take their research further by including information from the Bible story.

Give pairs a few minutes to read the information and create their montages, and then have them present the montages to the whole class.

ASK • **What does this information tell you about God?**

• **What does the information tell you about humans?**

• **According to your research, how do you think God wants us to treat each other?**

SAY **Let's learn more about Lot and Abram's division of the land.**

Historical Context | Genesis 13:1-18

Abram and Lot had gone south into Egypt because of a famine in the land of Canaan (Genesis 12:10). In Egypt Abram pretended to be Sarai's brother because Sarai was beautiful and he was afraid Pharaoh would kill him and take her. Pharaoh did have her brought into his palace, but he treated Abram very well, giving him sheep, cattle, servants, and a lot more. But then God began to inflict diseases on Pharaoh's household because of Sarai. When Pharaoh realized what was happening, he sent Abram and Sarai away. Abram, however, had apparently become a very wealthy man in the meantime. In fact, this is the first time Abram is described as having silver and gold (Genesis 13:2).

Abram and Lot headed north, back to the land God had promised to Abram's descendants. This was another long journey of about three hundred miles, again through rugged and barren territory, but nothing is mentioned of the trip in the Bible. A trip such as this would have to have been made in a series of short trips. The travelers would travel from one source of food and water to the next, but they would have to stay at each place long enough for the flocks and herds to recover from the deprivation they had suffered on the previous part of the journey.

Notice that while Abram was in Egypt, there is no indication that he prayed to God. That doesn't necessarily mean that he didn't pray. But we see that as soon as he returned to Canaan, he again "called on the name of the Lord." Perhaps the incident in Egypt reminded Abram of who God is, and of how blessed he was to have been chosen by God.

In Genesis 13:5 we discover for the first time that Lot was wealthy. Perhaps Abram had been generous to him, or maybe he, like Abram, had been successful in Egypt. At any rate, it became apparent that a single area was not sufficient to support both of their families' flocks and herds. Conflicts between their herdsmen over land use could have easily become quarrels between Abram and Lot (Genesis 13:8).

In this situation and culture, etiquette dictated that Lot allow Abram to take whatever he deemed was rightfully his, because Abram was the more powerful and wealthy as well as the respected elder. The aged were to be cared for and treated with respect. So Abram's offer probably shocked Lot—this was turning out far better than he had hoped! He had fully expected to end up with the harshest, least fertile part of the land, but here was his chance to get the fertile valley. Abram, to keep peace within his family, was willing to give up what was rightfully his. Lot, thinking only of himself, made a choice that his entire culture would have deemed unthinkable. The actions of these two men demonstrated the differences in their hearts.

After Lot left, God spoke again to Abram, expanding on the promise made earlier and no doubt reaffirming to Abram that he had done the right thing in keeping peace with Lot, even though for now he was stuck with inferior land. God's command to Abram to walk around the land must have grown out of the custom that a new landowner would walk the boundary of the land he was purchasing. God was telling Abram that he had given Abram that land.

Whose Sacrifice Is Greater?

Have teenagers get into groups of four, and give each group a Bible. Have groups read **Genesis 13:1-18** together.

ASK

- **How did Lot treat Abram?**
- **How did Abram treat Lot?**
- **Which one of these people made a sacrifice? Why did he make that sacrifice?**

• **Have you ever been faced with this type of decision? Explain.**

• **How should we treat others? Why?**

Distribute paper plates and markers.

SAY **Now I'd like you, in your groups, to brainstorm about the possible emotions each man in this story might have been feeling.**

Give groups a few moments to do this. After each group has thought of several emotions,

SAY **Now I'd like you to choose the most prevalent or important emotions that your group came up with and write each one on a separate paper plate.**

When groups have made their plates, ask a member of each group to share what the group wrote with the whole group.

When everyone has shared,

SAY **Now I'd like each group to create a real-life scenario about people who might be feeling the emotions written on the plates. For example, if your emotions are jealousy and greed, you might create a scenario about someone who has a really awesome possession and a friend of that person's who really wants that possession. You'll need to include your emotion plates in your scenario in some way. Once you've created a scenario, prepare to role play the scenario for the rest of the group.**

Give groups about five minutes to create their presentations, and then have them share their scenarios with the whole group. After the presentations are finished,

ASK • **How were these scenarios similar to the Bible story? How were they different?**

• **When have you ever found yourself in a situation like any of the situations in the scenarios we just saw? Explain.**

Givers and Takers

Give each group a Bible, a copy of the "Givers and Takers" handout (p. 96), and a pen.

SAY **I'd like you to look up the passages on the bottom of your handout. Each one of these passages involves someone giving and someone taking. Read the passages in your group, and then fill out the chart at the top of the handout—write all of the main characters in the first column, write the givers in the passage and what they gave**

Tip From the Trenches

Help your students understand that there are several instances throughout the Bible in which people dealt with the same types of emotions and situations that Abram and Lot did. Help your students discover that the people who God chose to note in his Word were normal people, just like them.

For Extra Impact

For an interesting twist on this activity, divide students into three groups. Give one group an Emily Post-type etiquette book, one group a *Robert's Rules of Order* book, and the third group a Bible. Have groups role play the exchange between Abram and Lot according to the information they think might be contained in the resources you've given them. Once groups have had the chance to role play, ask them which avenue they felt was most effective and why.

for Younger teenagers

You may want to move from group to group to see how younger teenagers are doing on the assignment. If a group is having trouble getting started, ask some starter questions.

for OLDER teenagers

Instead of providing older teenagers with passages to look up, give them Bible dictionaries, concordances, or chain-reference Bibles to use. Give students a brief study in the use of these resources, and have them look up their own passages under headings such as "selfishness" or "giving."

Tip From the Trenches

Make sure that your volunteers know that they don't need to record every response on their newsprint sheets. Each volunteer should write only responses that correspond to the title of his or her newsprint sheet. For example, Abram would be listed on the Givers sheet and not on the Takers sheet.

in the second column, write the takers in the passage and what they took in the third column, and write the result of the actions in the last column.

As groups are working, hang two sheets of newsprint on opposite ends of your meeting room. On one sheet write "Givers," and on the other write "Takers."

When groups are finished,

SAY **Now I need two volunteers to write responses on these newsprint sheets.**

Give each volunteer a marker.

SAY **I'd like a representative from each group to share the information your group wrote in the chart. Tell us who the main characters were, whether they were givers or takers, what they gave or took, and what the result was.**

After groups have shared,

ASK
- **What are the characteristics of the people who took?**
- **What are the characteristics of the people who gave?**
- **What emotions were the people in these passages wrestling with?**

- **How do you think the people listed on the Givers sheet feel about the way to treat other people? How about the people on the Takers sheet?**

Bible Application

I'm Here to Serve

Set out the rest of the doughnuts (or another snack), napkins, cups, and pitchers of juice. Have students line up facing away from you, and put a small piece of masking tape on each of their backs. Write either a 1 or a 2 on each piece of tape.

SAY **If you have a number 1 on your back, you are to serve the refreshments to other people. If you have a number 2 on your back, you are to wait for someone to serve you. Since you don't know what number is on your back, you'll need to guess what number you have on your back and act accordingly. You're not allowed to ask other students what your number is.**

Let students serve each other or wait to be served for a few minutes, and then reveal their numbers to them.

ASK
- **Did you have the number you thought you had?**

- **Did your actions change when you found out your number? How?**
- **Before you knew your number, how did you decide whether or not to serve others?**

SAY **Serving others is one action that demonstrates the way we should treat each other.**

ASK

- **What are some other good ways to demonstrate the way we should treat others?**

- **How can the way we treat others affect people who may be watching?**

Rating My Ability

SAY **Now I'd like you all to gather in the center of the room and look at the two sheets of newsprint. Sit down, and take a few moments to think about your tendency to either put others first or to put yourself first. Ask yourself the question,**

- **"How do I usually treat others?"**

When everyone has had time to think,

SAY **Think of the space between the newsprint sheets as an invisible rating area. I'd like you to rate your tendency to put other people first. If you think you do a good job, stand close to the Givers sheet. If you'd really like to work on your ability to put others before yourself, stand close to the Takers sheet.**

Give teenagers time to find their places, and then ask volunteers to share why they chose to stand where they are.

When teenagers have shared, give each teenager an index card and a pen. Read **Luke 6:31** aloud, and ask students to write the verse on their index cards.

SAY **Now I'd like you to bow your head and say the Key Verse to yourself several times. Then think of someone in your life you'd like to strive to put before yourself. This might be a friend, a younger brother or sister, or a parent. Then turn over your index card and write a short prayer, asking God to help you apply the Key Verse to your relationship with that person.**

Have students take their index cards home with them as reminders of the way God wants us to treat each other.

Tip From the Trenches

Be on the lookout for students who are sticking with their friends. Help them see that rating themselves in this activity is important. If you sense that some students are just sitting with their friends rather than truly assessing their own actions, ask them leading questions to help them evaluate more clearly how they treat others.

Tip From the Trenches

To help strengthen the connection between church and home, photocopy the "Taking It Home" page at the end of this study, and either distribute copies to students before they leave or mail them home. Encourage students to complete the reading, activities, and discussion with their families during the coming week.

Faith Journal

Give students each an index card and a pen. Have teenagers write their names and answers to the following question on their index cards:

- What does Abram's treatment of Lot tell you about the way God wants us to treat each other?

Have teenagers return their index cards to you. Before you meet with the group again, take some time to write personal responses to your students on their index cards. You may want to keep a notebook or a box containing copies of these index cards.

For more information about the Faith Journal option, refer to page 5 in the Introduction.

Music Connection

idea:listen

track 9:

Play "Forgive Forget." As the song is playing, have students think about ways the emotions and issues expressed in the song may parallel Lot and Abram's situation or situations in their lives. When the song is finished, have students share their thoughts.

ASK • **How might forgiveness be a way of putting other's needs ahead of your own?**

Have teenagers get into pairs, and use the issues and emotions expressed in the song to create a short scenario and dialogue that will demonstrate the way people should treat each other. Tell teenagers that they can draw from situations in their own lives or they can make up different situations. For example, a pair might create a scenario about two friends who are repairing their friendship after a fight.

Have teenagers present their dialogues to the class. Then have pairs read **Luke 6:27-36** together.

ASK • **How did you see the things listed in this Scripture shown in the Bible story today?**

• **How did you see the things listed in this Scripture demonstrated in the song?**

Have teenagers each choose one area of the Scripture that they'll commit to working on in their lives during the coming week. Then have pairs share a prayer together, asking God to help their partners use the knowledge in the Scripture in their relationships.

Forgive Forget

(recorded by Heather Miller)

Chorus

Forgive, forget—
You know it's all in the past.
Forgive, forget—
Let's make our promises last.
Forgive, forget—
There's nothing I'd rather be
Than free like a bird above the forgiveness sea.

I know you, you know me,
And we both know when we disagree.
The pain is clear; still I fight the tears
'Cause I won't let you get the best of me.

We want to stop with ourselves on top.
Oh, that's no way to his peace.
Got to let it go, pray that he will show us
How to really believe.

Forgive, forget—
You know it's all in the past.
Forgive, forget—
Let's make our promises last.
Forgive, forget—
There's nothing I'd rather be
Than free like a bird above the forgiveness sea.

It's over now, can't believe I've found
Just how good it can feel.
When I look at you,
You look at me—
This time we can agree.

Forgive, forget—
You know it's all in the past.
Forgive, forget—
Let's make our promises last.
Forgive, forget—
There's nothing I'd rather be
Than free like a bird above the forgiveness sea.

Forgive, forget—
Far as the east from the west.
Forgive, forget—
Let's put our faith to the test.
Forgive, forget—
There's nothing he'd rather do
Than lay an altar of peace between me and you.

Forgive, forget—
You know it's all in the past.
Forgive, forget—
Let's make our promises last.
Forgive, forget—
There's nothing he'd rather do
Than lay an altar of peace between me and you.

You gotta lay an altar of peace between me and you.

[music]

forgive

forget

Givers and Takers

idea:give & take

[t h i n k]

give and take

Main Characters	Givers and What They Gave	Takers and What They Took	Result

Scriptures:

Genesis 13:1-18
Matthew 25:31-46
Luke 9:10-17
Luke 21:1-4
John 13:2-20

Driving Home the Point:

The story is told of an old monastery that had fallen on hard times. Years earlier, it had been a thriving order that had a great influence. But now, all of the brothers were dying, and the few remaining were more than seventy years old. One day, one of the monks was walking in the woods, agonizing over the fate of his beloved monastery. He came across an old hermit who many believed to be a prophet. The monk decided to ask the hermit what could be done to save the monastery. The hermit thought for a moment and said, "The only thing I can tell you is that one of you is an apostle of God."

The monk hurried back to the monastery, eager to share his news with the other monks. In his haste, he forgot to ask the hermit which one of them was an apostle.

Upon hearing the news, the monks began to speculate about which of them it might be. As they contemplated, they began to treat each other with extraordinary respect and care on the off chance that one of them might be the apostle.

Soon, the people of the nearby village began to sense the aura of peace and respect that seemed to radiate from the monastery. As a result, many were drawn to the monastery and heard anew the good news.

Many young men decided to join the monastery as a result of this amazing outreach, and soon the monastery became again a place of great spiritual influence.

Talking At Home:

Read **1 John 3:16-20** together and discuss these questions:

- How did the monks demonstrate this Scripture passage?

- How would the way you treat others change if you thought one of them was an apostle of God?

Think about this: How can you put the needs of your parents and siblings ahead of your own? We challenge you to try it, even just for a day. Don't boldly announce what you're doing—just do it!

The Ride of a Lifetime

Genesis 15:1-18

10

God Makes a Covenant With Abram

 **key question:** What are God's plans like?

 **study focus:** Teenagers will learn that although God's plans for them may not always be easy to follow, they can trust that his plans are good.

key verse: " 'For I know the plans I have for you,' declares the Lord, 'plans to prosper you and not to harm you, plans to give you hope and a future.' " Jeremiah 29:11

A Look at the Study

Study Sequence	Minutes	What Students Will Do	Classroom Supplies
Getting Started	10 to 15	**Big Family Trip**—Make "plans" for a family road trip and compare their plans to God's plans for their lives.	Newsprint, markers, tape, colored stickers in four different colors, four U.S. maps, paper, pens
Bible Story Exploration	5 to 10	**God's Plan for Abram**—Explore background information about Abram's quest to discover God's plan for him.	"Historical Context" copies (p. 101), paper, pens
	15 to 20	**Abram's Journey**—Experience the Bible story and then compare Abram's experiences to their own.	Bibles, "Abram's Life" handouts (p. 106)
	5 to 10	**The Life of Fred**—Help a hypothetical person discover ways of finding God's will for his life.	Bibles, "A Case Study About Fred" copies (p. 103), pen
Bible Application	5 to 10	**My Trip**—Prayerfully reflect on God's plans for their lives.	Newsprint, markers, tape, index cards, pens
	up to 5	**Faith Journal**—Explore the Key Question and respond in writing.	Index cards, pens
Music Connection	5 to 10	**Encourager**—Explore ways they can encourage each other in seeking God's will. Use this option at an appropriate time in the study.	Bible, CD: "Encourager" (Track 10), CD player

Age-Level Insight

Teenagers want to be responsible for their own lives and make their own plans. However, they don't always have the experience and maturity to foresee the consequences of their plans. Guide students in making plans by helping them think through the consequences of all they undertake.

Last Week's Impact

As teenagers arrive, greet them warmly and ask follow-up questions to review last week's study and Key Verse. Ask questions such as: "Why does God want us to put others before ourselves?" and "Were you successful at putting the needs of family members ahead of your own? Explain."

If you used the Faith Journal option last week, take this time to return your students' index cards to them.

for OLDER teenagers

You may want to have older teenagers dig a little deeper into this opening experience by having them create their own "road maps" of their lives, detailing times they felt God at work in their lives and times they were aware of God's plans for them.

Getting Started

Big Family Trip

Choose four different destinations in the United States that are a long distance away from your church. For example, if you're in Dallas, Texas, one of your destinations might be Chicago, Illinois. Write the following directions on a sheet of newsprint and hang it where students can see it:

1. Pick the best route to reach your destination.
2. Plan where you'll make your pit stops (meals and sleeping).
3. Calculate the travel time involved based on a travel speed of sixty miles per hour.
4. What will you do to pass the time in the car? Come up with some car games to play that will keep you from getting on each others' nerves.

Give each student a colored sticker. Make sure that you use an equal amount of each color of sticker so you'll have four equal groups. Ask students to get into groups according to their sticker colors.

Give each group a U.S. map, paper, and pens, and assign each group one of the four destinations. Give groups five minutes to work through the directions on the newsprint sheet.

When groups are finished, have them present their results.

ASK
- **When was the last long trip that you took? Where did you go?**
- **Did you plan important stops in advance? What stops did you plan? Why did you plan those stops in advance?**
- **How are our trip plans like the plans that God has for our lives? How are they different?**

- **What are God's plans like?**

Bible Story Exploration

God's Plan for Abram

Have students stay in their groups from the previous activity. Give each student a copy of the "Historical Context" box (p. 101), a pen, and a blank piece of paper.

SAY **I'd like you to begin your examination of God's guidance of Abram by studying some background information. As you read the information I've given you in your groups, I'd like you to think about key points in Abram's journey. When**

you've finished reading, use the blank piece of paper to create a "life map" for Abram. Be sure to show all of the key points you discovered in the reading, as well as anything you remember from previous studies.

Give groups a few minutes to read the material and create their maps. Then have them share their maps with the class.

ASK • **Did you think it was easy or difficult to create your map? Explain.**

• **How well do you think your map would help someone understand God's guidance of Abram?**

for Younger teenagers

Younger teenagers would enjoy creating their own large maps on sheets of newsprint. Have them create their maps to scale.

Historical Context | Genesis 15:1-18

Abram had just returned from defeating a coalition of kings to rescue his nephew, Lot, and the Lord appeared to him in a vision. Notice that in Haran God simply spoke to Abram; later in Canaan God appeared before Abram; now God appeared in a lengthy vision. With each meeting, God's plan for Abram became a bit clearer.

Now God's first words to Abram were words of comfort. Abram had just won a big military victory; he wasn't likely afraid of any foes. What was bothering Abram, and what God addressed, was Abram's continuing lack of a son to be his heir. So in response to God's words of comfort, Abram poured out his heart. The name Abram used in his cry to God is literally "Lord of mercy." Abram was pleading with God to bless him in this one area in which he had not received God's promised blessing.

When God assured Abram by restating his promise that Abram would have his own son, Abram responded in faith. He believed God, and God declared him righteous because of his faith! Nothing that Abram could do in obedience to God could make him righteous, but his faith in God did!

To give Abram complete assurance, God made a covenant with him. In those days a covenant was a very serious thing. The cutting in half of animals described in Genesis 15:10 was to signify that the same would happen to any party breaking the covenant. Notice, however, that Abram wasn't asked to pass between the animals, which would have sealed his commitment to the covenant. Only God, symbolized by the smoking firepot and blazing torch, passed and sealed God's commitment to the covenant. Only God was required to fulfill the covenant.

Another interesting note is that each type of animal that was sacrificed was later used for a particular kind of sacrifice: the heifer for the Day of Atonement, the goat for certain festivals, the ram for a guilt offering, and the dove for purification.

God's listing of all the things that were to come for Abram's descendants accomplished at least two things: First, it confirmed that God's promise would come true because God could see the results more than four hundred years in the future. Second, it assured Abram that even though his people would endure hardship, they would eventually possess the land as God had promised. God assured Abram that he had a plan for his people—a good plan that was sure to come true!

Tip From the Trenches

Some of your students might get confused during this activity. Others might be tempted to stay with the same partner for each question. Remind students that they need to find different partners for each question because this helps them get to know and work with other students. Be on the lookout for kids who are confused about what you are asking them to do. Be available to help students move through this activity smoothly.

for Younger teenagers

To help younger teenagers experience this Bible passage, have them rewrite the conversation between God and Abram in modern language in their pairs. Then have them share their "translations" with the larger group.

for OLDER teenagers

Give older teenagers Bibles and concordances or other Bible reference books, and have them search for passages that might help someone like Fred on his or her quest for discovering God's will.

SAY **Now let's learn more about God's plan for Abram's life.**

Abram's Journey

Ask kids to stay in their groups of four. Give each student a Bible and an "Abram's Life" handout (p. 106), and have groups read **Genesis 15:1-18** together.

When groups have read the passage,

SAY **Now I'm going to read a few verses from this passage to you again. When I finish reading a verse, I'd like you to find a partner from another group. Discuss with your partner the statement on your handout that goes with the verse I just read.**

Begin by reading **Genesis 15:1**, and then ask students to each find a partner and discuss the corresponding statement. Once pairs have discussed the statement, instruct students to return to their original groups and share what their partners said. Continue in this manner through the rest of the verses on the handouts, allowing students to find different partners for each question.

ASK
- **How would you feel if you were Abram? Explain.**
- **How did Abram know that God's plan for him was good?**
- **How much of God's plan did Abram know when he believed God?**
- **How would you feel if God told you that his plan for you would include times of extreme hardship?**

- **How can we know what God's plans for us are like?**

Read **Jeremiah 29:11** aloud to your group, emphasizing the phrase "For I know the plans I have for you."

ASK
- **Do you think Abram believed that God had good plans for him? Explain.**
- **Is this an easy verse for you to believe? Why or why not?**
- **How do you think your life might be different if you really, truly believed what this verse had to say?**

SAY **God has your life mapped out, and he wants you to trust his plans for you.**

The Life of Fred

Have teenagers return to their groups of four, and give each group a copy of "A Case Study About Fred" (p. 103) and a pen. Instruct groups to read the case study and answer the questions.

When groups are finished, ask them to share their answers.

ASK
- **Have you ever faced a situation like this one?**

A Case Study About Fred

Fred is confused. He's convinced that God has called him to something. His youth pastor has told him that God has a plan and that he needs to pursue whatever it is that God has called him to.

Here's the problem: Fred is confused about how to go about finding God's will. He's open to your suggestions. Since he's willing to try anything, whatever you suggest will be taken seriously.

Here's what you need to do:

- Suggest some steps Fred can take to discover God's plan for his life.
- Suggest some things that will help Fred on his journey to find God's will.
- Share with Fred your own search for God's plan.
- Use **Jeremiah 29:11** to encourage Fred.

- **What difficulties do you face as you search for God's plan for your life?**
- **Should you actively search for God's will or wait for him to tell you what to do? Explain.**
- **As you search for God's will, what other good things might happen?**

Bible Application

My Trip

Write the following questions on a sheet of newsprint, and tape the newsprint where students can see it:

1. What's at the top of your list of big plans for your life?
2. What do you think God has called you to do?
3. What's the best way to pursue God's plans for your life?
4. How should you act as you are getting to where God has called you?

For Extra Impact

Help your teenagers understand the concept of trusting God's plan by using this object study. You'll need two cinder blocks and one eight-foot 2x4 piece of wood. Place the cinder blocks exactly four feet apart, and ask a student to stand on one of the cinder blocks and describe how standing on the block feels. The student might share that the block feels solid or maybe that it feels higher but it still feels secure. Next, place the 2x4 on the cinder blocks, and ask another student to stand in the center of the wood. (Make sure you provide a spotter for the student standing on the 2x4.) Have the student share how secure he or she feels standing on the wood.

ASK
- **How is this experience like trusting God?**

Explain that trusting God's plans for the future feels the same way. God's plans and promises can be trusted; they're secure like a cinder block, not flimsy or untrustworthy like a weak piece of wood.

for Younger teenagers

To help younger teenagers get into a more reflective mood, you may want to play soothing, quiet music in the background and have them sit apart from each other.

Give each student a pen and an index card, and have students write the answers to the questions on their index cards. Give students time to think and pray silently. Allow students to leave quietly when they are finished. Have students take their index cards with them.

Faith Journal

Give students each an index card and a pen. Have teenagers write their names and answers to the following questions on their index cards:

- What did you learn about determining God's will for your life? How do you think you will apply this knowledge to your life now?

Have teenagers return their index cards to you. Before you meet with the group again, take some time to write personal responses to your students on their index cards. You may want to keep a notebook or a box containing copies of these index cards.

For more information about the Faith Journal option, refer to page 5 in the Introduction.

Teacher Skillbuilder

Your students are uncertain about the future. Invest your time helping them understand that God's plans for them are good and perfect and that God has made the same serious commitment to them as the commitment he made to Abram.

Tip From the Trenches

To help strengthen the connection between church and home, photocopy the "Taking It Home" page at the end of this study, and either distribute copies to students before they leave or mail them home. Encourage students to complete the reading, activities, and discussion with their families during the coming week.

Music Connection

track 10:

Read **Romans 1:11-12** aloud, and then play the song "Encourager." As the song is playing, have students identify ways in which the song demonstrates ways one person might encourage another in seeking God's plans. After the song,

ASK
- **What did you hear in this song and the Bible verses about ways we can encourage each other in seeking God's will?**
- **How was Abram encouraged in his journey toward God?**

Have students form pairs, and have partners each identify one area of their lives in which they are struggling right now with knowing God's will. Have partners think of specific ways they can encourage each other, and then have them commit to following through by encouraging each other during the coming week.

Encourager

(recorded by Glisten)

I'm not the one
With the masters plan,
And that may be hard for you to
Understand.
I'm not content
Just to sit on my hands;
I'm on my way to the Promised Land.

I've got places to go,
Choices to make,
No time to lose,
And old habits to break.
I'm pressing on;
I'm pressing in.
I will never stop,
Never give in.

You're on my side.
(You're on my side.)
You're on my side.

You're on my side.
(You're on my side.)
You're on my side.

Abram's Life

idea:experiences

[t h i n k]

Genesis / beginning

- **Genesis 15:1—God is our protector and our reward.**
Describe a time you knew you needed God's protection.

- **Genesis 15:5—God makes big promises.**
Describe a time God promised you something really huge.

- **Genesis 15:6—We're called righteous for believing God.**
Describe a time you believed one of God's big plans for you.

- **Genesis 15:13—God's plan could include uncomfortable moments.**
Describe a time when, in the process of following God, you felt like you were in spiritual, emotional, or physical captivity.

Driving Home the Point:

"I'm a cautious person. I'm more apt to 'just say no' than to 'just do it!' There are times when that attitude is OK, when it keeps me safe from harm. But other times it prevents me from experiencing much of what life—or God—has to offer.

"See, my caution carries over to my spiritual life. I am reluctant to give complete control of my life to God. I want to hear God only when it is convenient; I want to follow God only when I like where God is leading me; I want to serve God only when I have extra time.

"God knows what is best for us and what will make us the happiest; we have only to follow this call. Are you hesitant, as I am? I challenge you to hear God's call. I challenge you to answer. I challenge you to give in to God. Let's just do it!" **(Devo'Zine, July/August 1998)**

Talking At Home:

Read **Psalm 62:8** together and discuss these questions:

• When are some times that you've been afraid to "just do it"?

• How could the verse help you do the things you feel God is calling you to do?

• How can you know what God's plans are for you?

What kinds of things do you think God might be calling you to do? Make a list, and show it to your parents (yes, they do have good comments and ideas!). If you feel comfortable, take the list to others who know you, including youth leaders, teachers, friends, and relatives.

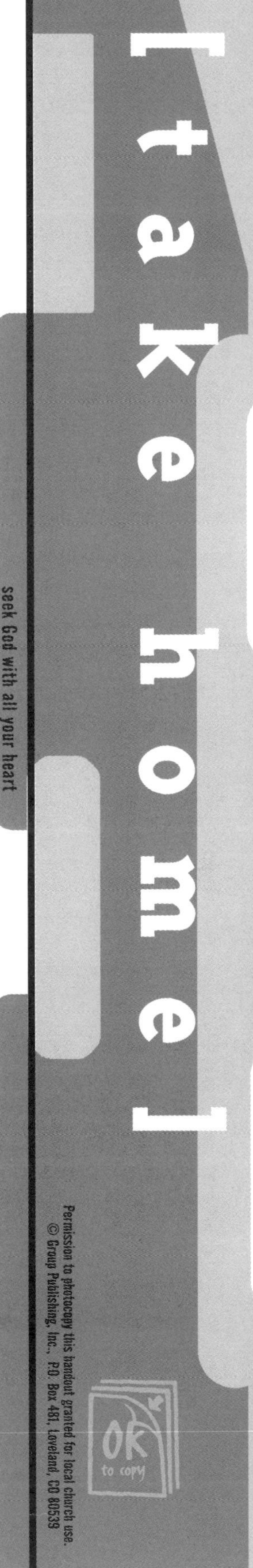

Caution—God at Work!

Genesis 18:1–19:29

11

Abraham Has Three Visitors

 **key question:** Why do miracles happen?

 **study focus:** Teenagers will learn that God does amazing things because of his goodness and mercy.

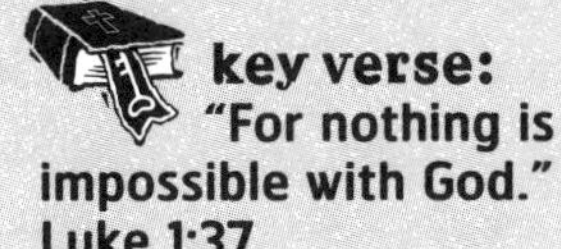 **key verse:** "For nothing is impossible with God." Luke 1:37

A Look at the Study

Study Sequence	Minutes	What Students Will Do	Classroom Supplies
Getting Started	5 to 10	**Miraculous Bingo**—Play a Bingo game detailing their knowledge of and experiences with miracles.	"Miraculous Bingo" handouts (p. 116), pens
	5 to 10	**Miracle Diplomats**—Create new words and definitions to explain what miracles are.	"Miraculous Bingo" handouts (p. 116), pens
Bible Story Exploration	5 to 10	**God Shows Himself Through Miracles**—Explore background information about the miracles in Abraham's life.	Bibles, "Historical Context" copies (p. 111), pens
	10 to 15	**My Favorite Miracle**—Experience the Bible story and create talk shows to share their findings.	Bibles, newsprint, markers
	5 to 10	**God's Miraculous Works**—Explore many of God's miracles in the Bible and brainstorm ways God intervenes in our lives today.	Bibles, "The Word on Miracles" handouts (p. 116), pencils, newsprint, markers, tape
Bible Application	5 to 10	**Miracles for Me**—Use the Key Verse in letters to God.	Bible, paper, pens
	up to 5	**Faith Journal**—Explore the Key Question and respond in writing.	Index cards, pens
Music Connection	5 to 10	**Doctor in the House**—Explore modern miracles. Use this option at an appropriate time in the study.	Bibles, CD: "Doctor in the House" (Track 11), CD player

Age-Level Insight

The fact that God does amazing things may not even enter into the thinking of today's teenager. Perhaps when a difficult situation arises, he or she might covet God's miraculous action. But teenagers don't necessarily expect miracles or see God's amazing power around them until they're brought up short by something unexpected. An experience with nature or the experience of coming through a difficult time intact may spur teenagers to think seriously about God's amazing power and how he uses it in love. Be watchful for those types of situations in the lives of teenagers. Help them to understand and experience the amazing things God does every day.

Getting Started

Miraculous Bingo

Photocopy and cut apart the handouts on page 116, and give each student a "Miraculous Bingo" handout and a pen. Instruct teenagers to mingle and try to score Bingo wins on their handouts by finding people who can answer the questions.

Give students a few minutes to mingle. When the time is up, have teenagers share squares they weren't able to complete. Cheer for teenagers who were able to make Bingo scores.

ASK • **What is a miracle?**

- **Do you believe in miracles? Why or why not?**
- **Have you experienced a miracle firsthand? Explain.**

- **Why do you think miracles happen?**

Miracle Diplomats

Ask students to get into groups of no larger than four.

SAY **You've been sent by your church to share your faith with people who live in remote parts of Africa. While you're in Africa, the people you're working with hear you talking about the amazing things God has done. However, they have no idea what a miracle is. Your job is to come up with a new word and a definition for the word that will explain what a miracle is.**

Give groups three minutes to come up with their words and definitions and write them on the backs of their "Miraculous Bingo" handouts (p. 116). When groups are done, have them present their words and definitions to the rest of the group.

ASK

- **Why do miracles happen?**

- **Do you have to experience a miracle in order to understand it? Why or why not?**
- **Do miracles happen only to people who believe in God? Explain.**

SAY **God's wonderful and amazing deeds are recorded in his Word. Getting acquainted with God's Word will help you to fully understand why miracles happen. Let's look into God's Word and read about some amazing events that affected people differently.**

Last Week's Impact

As teenagers arrive, greet them warmly and ask follow-up questions to review last week's study and Key Verse. Ask questions such as "What insights did your parents give you about God's plans for you?" and "How can you learn more about God's plans?"

If you used the Faith Journal option last week, take this time to return your students' index cards to them.

for Younger teenagers

To get younger teenagers started, you may want to have them define the components of a miracle. You might also want to have them brainstorm miracles they're aware of to help them discover what the miracles have in common.

Historical Context | Genesis 18:1–19:29

Since the story covered in last week's study, Abram, whose name meant "exalted father," has gone through the covenant of circumcision, and God has renamed him Abraham, "father of many." God also renamed Sarai. Her new name, Sarah, stressed that she was to be the mother of nations and kings and thus serve the Lord's purpose.

In Abraham's desert-dwelling culture, visitors were rare. They provided both an obligation and a welcome diversion. A warm welcome and hospitality were requirements in the culture of that day, and Abraham knew what it was like to travel in the desert. Thus, he was ready to warmly welcome the travelers, and the travelers were probably just as eager for conversation as Abraham.

It may seem strange that the three men were "standing nearby" (Genesis 18:2), but this was customary for strangers in that time and place. They were not free to just approach someone else's tent in the desert.

Many scholars believe that these men were angels, though the text doesn't directly say so. The fact that they knew Sarah's name may support the idea that they were angels, and in Genesis 18:10, it becomes clear that one of them was at least speaking for the Lord.

For many years, God had been promising a son. Now for the first time, God predicted the time of the birth to ninety-nine-year-old Abraham and eighty-nine-year-old Sarah: Within one year, the son of the promise would be born. Sarah's laughter is understandable. Who would have thought that a ninety-year-old woman could have a baby! God does truly amazing things!

When God made it clear that his intent was to destroy Sodom and Gomorrah, Abraham was horrified. No doubt he had done business with people there, and his nephew, Lot, lived there with his family. So Abraham pleaded with God to spare the few who were still faithful. Notice that God's response was not to spare just the righteous; God said the whole city would be saved if only fifty righteous people lived there. It's helpful to remember here God's definition of "righteous." Abraham was declared righteous because of his faith, not because of a righteous lifestyle. As Abraham voiced his pleas ever more carefully, God promised to spare the city if only ten righteous people could be found there. However, there weren't even ten faithful people there.

Lot's position at the gate to the city indicated that he was a man of influence there, perhaps even a judge. His insistence that the visitors stay at his home was almost a requirement of the culture. The moral degradation of this city is obvious in the text, so no further comment is needed here. Lot apparently was at least somewhat involved in what was happening in the culture, as evidenced by his offering of his daughters to the men who were seeking sex with the visitors.

God did an amazing thing in sparing the lives of Lot and his family. Lot didn't appear to deserve it, just as we don't deserve the grace God gives to us. But we can be thankful that God is wonderfully merciful and still does amazing things for us.

God Shows Himself Through Miracles

Give each student a copy of the "Historical Context" box (p. 111), a Bible, and a pen.

SAY **I'd like you to begin your study of the miracles in Abraham's life by studying some background information. As you read the information I've given you, I'd like you to be focusing on miracles in the material. When you're finished reading, I'd like you to go back through the material you read and circle all of the miracles you read about.**

Give pairs a few minutes to read the information and circle the miracles, and then have them share the miracles they found with the whole class.

ASK
- **Did you all agree on what constituted a miracle? Why or why not?**
- **What does this information tell you about God?**

- **Based on your research, why do you think miracles happen?**

SAY **Let's learn more about God's miracles in Abraham's life.**

My Favorite Miracle

On three separate sheets of newsprint, write "A Wonderful Gift—**Genesis 18:1-15**;" "A Changed Mind—**Genesis 18:16-33**;" and "Total Destruction—**Genesis 19:1-29**."

Divide teenagers into three equal groups, and give each group a Bible and markers. Assign each group a sheet of newsprint. Ask groups to write the words "Amazing Event," "Cause," and "Reaction" on their newsprint sheets. Give groups five minutes to read their passages, and then have them answer the questions "Who?" "What?" "When?" "Where?" and "How?" about their passages on their newsprint sheets.

When groups are done researching, have each group create a talk show to present its findings. Each talk show must include a host or hostess who interviews each of the main characters involved in the story. Have students act as either the host or hostess or the guests, and have groups come up with possible interview questions ahead of time using the information on their newsprint sheets. Encourage groups to use their creativity to see the amazing events they read about from their characters' perspectives.

Allow groups about ten minutes to create and present their talk shows.

When all groups have presented,

ASK

- **According to your research, why do miracles happen?**
- **Is a miracle always a positive event? Why?**
- **Does a person or event have to be physically changed in order to experience a miracle? Why or why not?**

Teacher Skillbuilder

This study deals with a subject that's somewhat difficult. Miracles, amazing happenings, and divine interventions have become more "popular" in today's media. Your teenagers are wrestling with the factuality of miracles. On one hand, they want to believe that God intervenes in their world. On the other hand, if they're vocal about their beliefs, they run the risk of being labeled fanatics. Use this study to provide a safe environment for students' discussions about miracles. Help your teenagers understand that miracles happen because God wants to intervene and possibly change their lives.

for Younger teenagers

If a group is having trouble getting started, ask some starter questions, such as "What's happening in your passage?" or "Who's involved in the story?"

For Extra Impact

Videotape the students' talk shows, and show them to other groups in the church.

God's Miraculous Works

Have teenagers form groups of four, and give each group a "The Word on Miracles" handout section (p. 116) and a pencil. Ask each group to pick a leader, and have members of each group lay the group's handout section face up on the floor and gather around it. Have leaders drop their pencils, tips down, on the handouts. Each group will read the passage that the leader's pencil marks.

When groups have read their passages, have each group member join with one person from another group. Have partners tell each other about their passages.

When pairs have shared, ask them to brainstorm ways that God intervenes in our lives today. Give each pair newsprint and markers to record their ideas.

When pairs are done,

- **What evidence suggests that God is finished doing miracles?**
- **What, if anything, is different about the miracles God performs today?**

- **Why do miracles happen today?**

Ask pairs to hang their lists on a designated wall in your meeting room.

For Extra Impact

Try videotaping various segments of popular Christian TV broadcasts. Many of them have segments in which God physically, mentally, or emotionally heals people. Once you've shown these segments to your teenagers, ask them to share how the stories make them feel. Ask them to consider the validity of the miracles that take place.

Bible Application

Miracles for Me

Have teenagers walk around and read the brainstorming lists. When students have looked at the lists, read the Key Verse (**Luke 1:37**) aloud.

Have teenagers sit quietly and think about someone who might need a miracle. Distribute paper and pens or pencils. Ask teenagers each to write a letter to God asking for a miracle for someone they love. Have students begin their letters with the phrase, "Dear God, because nothing is impossible for you..." Have students complete the sentence with their requests for miracles.

When teenagers are finished writing, have volunteers share their letters.

Close by praying together for the needs your teenagers have mentioned in their letters.

Faith Journal

Give students each an index card and a pen. Have teenagers write their names and answers to the following question on their index cards:

- Why do you think God sometimes chooses to communicate with people through miracles?

Tip From the Trenches

To help strengthen the connection between church and home, photocopy the "Taking It Home" page at the end of this study, and either distribute copies to students before they leave or mail them home. Encourage students to complete the reading, activities, and discussion with their families during the coming week.

Have teenagers return their index cards to you. Before you meet with the group again, take some time to write personal responses to your students on their index cards. You may want to keep a notebook or a box containing copies of these index cards.

For more information about the Faith Journal option, refer to page 5 in the Introduction.

Music Connection

track 11:
Tell students you're going to play the song "Doctor in the House." As they listen, have them think about the miracles they hear in the song. When the song is finished, have them share their thoughts. Then have one volunteer read **Mark 2:1-12**, and have another volunteer read **Mark 8:22-26**.

ASK • **Do you think miracles like these still happen today? Explain.**

Share the following account of a modern miracle with your students:

"A young mother was standing at the kitchen sink washing dishes one spring morning...As she looked out the window into the backyard, she noticed that the garden gate had been left open. Her little three-year-old daughter, Lisa, had toddled through the gate and was sitting casually on the railroad tracks playing with the gravel. The mother's heart stopped when she saw a train coming around the bend and heard its whistle blaring persistently. As she raced from the house screaming her daughter's name, she suddenly saw a striking figure, clothed in pure white, lifting Lisa off the tracks. While the train roared past, this glorious being stood by the track with an arm around the child. Together, they watched the train go by. When the mother reached her daughter's side, Lisa was standing alone."

(Hope MacDonald, "In a Moment of Time," published in *Unsolved Miracles*)

ASK • **Have you ever experienced a miracle (or do you know someone who has)? Explain.**

• **Why do you think God sometimes chooses to show himself through miracles in our lives?**

Encourage students to share personal stories and testimonies about miracles in their lives.

Doctor in the House

(recorded by B.O.B)

Standin' on the side of the road—
Crowd is passing by.
But I can only hear them;
See, I'm blind in both eyes.
So I'm yellin' at the top of my lungs—
"Somebody help me now!"
So they brought a man before me,
And I didn't know how
He could make a difference.
And was it gonna hurt?
The next thing I know,
He was spittin' in the dirt.

Chorus: (repeat three times)
Is there a doctor in the house?
Check it!

They said I'd never walk again—
I was flat on my back.
I got carried to a meeting.
Oh, but the place was packed!
So my friends cut a hole in the roof,
And they lowered me on down,
Right in front of the man
Who was the talk of the town.
I had nothin' to lose;
I wondered what he'd say.
He pointed to my stretcher;
He said, "Throw that away!"

Chorus: (repeat seven times)
Is there a doctor in the house?
Hey, hey, hey, hey!

When the pain won't go away,
I get on my knees and pray.
In my condition,
I need a Great Physician—
The One who knows how I was made.

Chorus: (repeat twelve times)
Is there a doctor in the house?
Hey!

[music]

miracles

Miraculous Bingo

idea:miracles

[t h i n k]

Someone who has a friend that needs a miracle.	*Someone who has never seen a miracle. Ask this person to share what he or she thinks a miracle would be like.*	*Someone who can tell you what a miracle is.*	*Someone who doesn't like Miracle Whip on his or her sandwiches.*
Someone who has experienced a miracle firsthand.	*Someone who wants a miracle. Have him or her tell you why.*	*Three people who will sing, "I need a miracle today" to the tune of "Happy Birthday."*	*Someone who likes sushi. (Ask if you can smell his or her breath!)*
Someone who has had a really rough week. Have him or her share what it was like.	*Three people who will make a pyramid and shout, "God is amazing!"*	*Free Space* *Anyone can sign his or her name here.*	*Someone who has seen a miracle happen.*
Find someone who has no idea what a miracle is, and do your best to describe one to him or her.	*Someone who can stand on his or her head and say the word "miracle" ten times fast.*	*Someone who likes Miracle Whip on his or her sandwiches.*	*Someone who knows where a miracle is in God's Word.*

diagonal

cut here

The Word on Miracles

Old Testament	New Testament
Genesis 2:4-22	Matthew 8:2-4
Genesis 11:1-8	Matthew 8:23-27
Exodus 3:1-6	Mark 1:23-26
Exodus 8:20-24	Mark 6:48-51
Exodus 14:13-28	Luke 17:11-19
Joshua 10:1-14	Luke 22:50-51
1 Kings 17:1-6	John 2:1-11
1 Kings 19:9-14	John 11:1-44
Ezekiel 2:9–3:4	Acts 3:1-8
Daniel 5:5-17	Acts 10:9-16

Talking About It idea:discuss

Driving Home the Point:

"The miracles in fact are a retelling in small letters of the very same story which is written across the whole world in letters too large for some of us to see." **(C.S. Lewis)**

Talking At Home:

Read **Psalm 77:13-15** together and discuss these questions:

- Do you think God still performs miracles today? Explain.

- Why do you think God chooses to show himself through miracles?

Read through the following list of passages:

Old Testament	New Testament
Genesis 2:4-22	Matthew 8:2-4
Genesis 11:1-8	Matthew 8:23-27
Exodus 3:1-6	Mark 1:23-26
Exodus 8:20-24	Mark 6:48-51
Exodus 14:13-28	Luke 17:11-19
Joshua 10:1-14	Luke 22:50-51
1 Kings 17:1-6	John 2:1-11
1 Kings 19:9-14	John 11:1-44
Ezekiel 2:9–3:4	Acts 3:1-8
Daniel 5:5-17	Acts 10:9-16

Survey the thoughts of your family members about miracles.

Why Should I Be Happy?

Genesis 21:1-6

12

Isaac Is Born

 **key question:** How should we respond to God's gifts?

 **study focus:** Teenagers will learn to respond with joy to the gifts God gives.

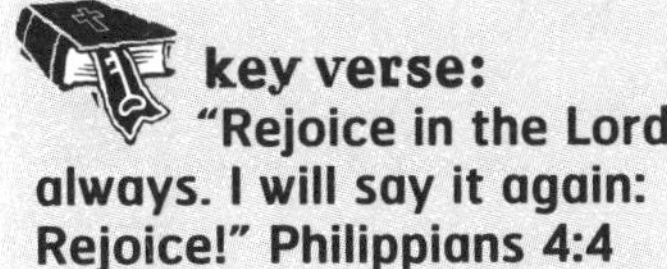

key verse: "Rejoice in the Lord always. I will say it again: Rejoice!" Philippians 4:4

A Look at the Study

Study Sequence	Minutes	What Students Will Do	Classroom Supplies
Getting Started	5 to 10	**Surprise!**—Create definitions of joy and be surprised with a party.	Party supplies, newsprint, tape, markers
	15 to 20	**Hunt for Joy**—Go on an "interview hunt" in which they'll interview people about the gifts God has given them.	Paper, pens, newsprint, tape, marker
Bible Story Exploration	5 to 10	**Sarah's Surprise**—Explore background information about the birth of Isaac.	"Historical Context" copies (p. 122), paper, pens
	10 to 15	**You're Pregnant?**—Explore modern-day versions of Sarah's pregnancy and compare what they discovered to the Bible story.	Bibles, "A Strange Event" handouts (p. 126), pens
Bible Application	5 to 10	**Jazzed About Joy**—Reflect on God's gifts and their responses, and then create a cheer using the Key Verse.	Newsprint, markers, tape
	up to 5	**Faith Journal**—Explore the Key Question and respond in writing.	Index cards, pens
Music Connection	5 to 10	**Rejoice**—Identify gifts in their lives and ways to thank God for those gifts. Use this option at an appropriate time in the study.	Newsprint, markers, CD: "Rejoice" (Track 12), CD player

Age-Level Insight

Sometimes teenagers see happiness as their ultimate goal in life, and sometimes they see God and adults as the major roadblocks to achieving that goal. Encourage them to talk about the things that they think bring joy and happiness. Encourage them to be candid with you. Help them to discover that God's wish for them is to live joyful lives, and help them to discover where such joy comes from.

Last Week's Impact

As teenagers arrive, greet them warmly and ask follow-up questions to review last week's study and Key Verse. Ask questions such as "Have you seen any miracles this week? Explain," and "Why does God sometimes choose to reveal himself through miracles?"

If you used the Faith Journal option last week, take this time to return your students' index cards to them.

For Extra Impact

If you're using this study the Sunday before Thanksgiving, you may want to make your party a Thanksgiving surprise party.

Tip From the Trenches

Timing for this activity is important. Make sure that you have your signal worked out with your adults. Also, it could be very easy for this opener to take over the rest of the study. Ask the adults to help keep students in their trios and focused.

Getting Started

Surprise!

Before the study, ask adults to help you with a surprise party for students. Ask them to stay out of sight until you give them the signal. When you give the signal, they're to burst into the room and begin the surprise party. Be sure to give them party supplies, including refreshments, party horns and hats, balloons, and confetti.

To prepare for the study, hang a sheet of newsprint on a wall, and scatter markers near it.

Before giving the signal,

SAY **I'd like you to form trios and sit down in your trios. Each trio needs to create a definition of the word "joy." When you've come up with a definition, one person from your trio needs to write the definition on the newsprint.**

Give students about thirty seconds to work.

SAY **Today we're going to look at the gifts God gives us. We'll see that...**[give the signal for adults to come in and interrupt].

Spend the next five minutes helping teenagers get their party food and drinks. As students get their food, ask them to sit with their trios. When everyone has received food, ask trios to share their definitions of joy with the whole group.

ASK
- **How did it feel to be surprised this way?**
- **Does your trio's definition of joy describe the way you are feeling right now?**
- **What types of things give you the most joy?**

- **Does receiving a gift from God give you joy? Why?**

Allow time for teenagers to discuss these questions in their trios. When they're done, ask volunteers to share their responses with the rest of the class.

Hunt for Joy

Gather students together.

SAY **Now I'd like you, in your trios, to go on an impromptu interview hunt. This is kind of like a scavenger hunt, except you'll be collecting interviews. Each trio will need to find at least two other people who aren't in this class. You'll need to ask each person to tell you about a time he or she has received a gift from God.**

Give paper and pens to each trio.

SAY **Before you go on your interview hunt, I'd like you to come up with a few interview questions. Make sure that you get the person's name, the gift he or she received, and how he or she felt about the gift. You have ten minutes to collect your interviews.**

While you're waiting for students to return, write the following gift types on a sheet of newsprint, and tape the newsprint to the wall:

• A gift the person needed (such as the resolution of a serious situation or a new place to live);

• A gift the person wasn't expecting (such as an anniversary gift).

When students have returned,

SAY **Please sit with your trio in the center of the meeting space.**

When students are seated,

SAY **Now, each trio needs to choose a spokesperson to share with us a summary of the trio's interviews.**

Show students the newsprint sheet.

SAY **While you're listening to the interview summaries, keep track of the number of each type of gift you hear about in the interviews.**

When all of the interview summaries have been shared, have students share their totals for each type of gift.

ASK
- **What did you notice about people's responses when they were given gifts?**
- **How do you respond when you're given a gift?**
- **Which is better: a gift from your parents or a gift from God? Why?**

- **How do you think we should respond to God's gifts?**

Bible Story Exploration

Sarah's Surprise

Divide the class into two groups, and give each group a copy of the "Historical Context" box (p. 122), paper, and pens.

SAY **I'd like you to begin your exploration of the story of Sarah's surprise by learning some historical background**

For Extra Impact

Give each trio a video camera and a videotape to capture the interviews. Make sure that you have a television and a videocassette recorder to play responses for the entire group.

for Younger teenagers

For younger teenagers, you may want to provide more direction and guidance for this activity. For example, you might want to help students come up with good interview questions and have them practice on each other before sending them out on their "hunts."

Tip From the Trenches

If other classes and people aren't available, have students interview each other (and you), or have them conduct brief telephone interviews with church members.

information. In your group, you'll need to read through the information and then create a brief "you were there" story. Act as if you were there to observe what was happening to Abraham and Sarah. Be sure to include your identity as an observer and any fun details you can think of.

Give groups a few minutes to read through their information and create their stories. Then have groups share their stories with the whole class, one at a time.

After they're finished,

ASK
- **What was one interesting fact you learned from another group's story?**
- **What does the information you just learned about tell you about God?**

- **What does the information tell you about what our response should be to God's gifts?**

for Younger teenagers

Younger teenagers might enjoy creating role-plays or short skits of their stories and presenting them to the class.

Historical Context | Genesis 21:1-6

God keeps his promises. In the first two verses of this passage, three times we read that God did what he said he would do. For Abraham and Sarah, it was the miraculous fulfillment of an amazing promise: the birth of a son to ninety- and one-hundred-year-old parents who had never before been able to have a child! And it was really *their* child—the son of both Abraham and Sarah—as confirmed in Genesis 21:2-3. The shame of childlessness that had haunted them for decades was finally erased. God brought a kind of joy to Abraham and Sarah that they had never known.

"Isaac," the name Abraham gave his son, means "he laughs." God had told Abraham to give the child that name a year or more earlier (Genesis 17:19). God apparently wanted Abraham and Sarah to remember that they had both laughed at different times in response to God's announcement that they would have a son at their advanced ages (Genesis 17:17; 18:12). And perhaps God also wanted the name to remind them in the years to come of the joy God had brought them.

The circumcision of Isaac when he was eight days old wasn't done just in obedience to God's command. It was a sign of the covenant between God and Abraham, a sign that this child was one of God's chosen people (Genesis 17:10-14).

Genesis 21:6 contains a play on words that's pretty obvious even in English. Through the child named "he laughs," God had brought laughter to Sarah and to all who knew her. In those days, any birth of a healthy child brought great joy, even more so if it was a boy. But a firstborn son, born to such elderly parents, was certainly a laughing matter! Sarah could hardly contain her happiness. Who could blame her?

Twenty-five years had passed since Abraham had left his home in Ur of the Chaldeans to follow God. Twenty-five years had passed since God first promised to make Abraham's descendants into a great nation. Twenty-five years had passed since a childless couple of sixty-five and seventy-five years of age first believed God's promise that they would have children. What a fantastic mountaintop in Abraham and Sarah's faith journey! "He Laughs" was born!

SAY **Now let's learn more about the gift God gave to Abraham and Sarah.**

You're Pregnant?

SAY **Now we're going to explore a different kind of gift.**

Give each student "A Strange Event" handout (p. 126) and a pen. Divide the class into four groups, and give each group a Bible. Assign each group one of the situations on the handout.

SAY **Together with the members of your group, I'd like you to write a complete story about your assigned situation. Make sure to give plenty of details in your story. Use the back of one of your handouts. I'll give you five minutes to write your story.**

When groups are finished, begin by having a volunteer from group 1 read the group's story aloud. Then proceed to groups 2, 3, and 4.

SAY **The stories you wrote sound impossible. Let's look at how God did something very similar. Please pay attention to the reaction people had to this unusual gift.**

Ask groups to read **Genesis 21:1-6.**

ASK • **How do you think Abraham and Sarah must have felt?**

• **How do you think you would feel in a situation like this?**

• **How do you think you would have responded to this gift from God?**

• **If you could write a definition for the word "joy" from Abraham and Sarah's perspective, what would you write?**

Bible Application

Jazzed About Joy

Write the following statements on newsprint taped to the wall.

• One of the best gifts God has given me is...

• **My response to that gift was...**

SAY **I'd like you to read these statements and then sit quietly and think about your responses to them.**

Give students a minute to think .

For Extra Impact

Help your teenagers understand the real impact of what Sarah and Abraham were feeling by inviting a couple who have just had a baby to discuss their feelings about being new parents. Make sure that you brief them in advance about the passage, and be sure to have them focus on the joy of the miracle of birth. Also, you may want to give them a time limit so their speech doesn't prolong your study.

Teacher Skillbuilder

Some teenagers seldom feel happy and think they have nothing to feel joyful about. For these students, this study may feel like salt in an open wound. How will you know if you're talking about something that is making a few of your students uncomfortable? Look for students who act up and disrupt during this study or those who retreat and don't want to be a part of this study. It's essential that you're aware of your students' reactions both during and after this study. Look for students who may be genuinely unhappy, and be ready to listen to their hurts. The Faith Journal responses will give you an insight into students' lives as well.

SAY **Now I'd like you each to share one of your responses with the class. After every response, I'm going to read Philippians 4:4 aloud, and then I'd like you to stand and cheer. If you know the verse or if you pick it up after I've said it a few times, say it with me.**

Have students share their responses one at a time, and after each one, read the Key Verse and have the group stand and cheer.

When everyone has had a chance to share, close the meeting with a prayer thanking God for the many gifts he gives us and the opportunity to praise him.

Faith Journal

Give students each an index card and a pen. Have teenagers write their names and answers to the following question on their index cards:

• What are some ways you could express a joyful response to God's tremendous gifts to you?

Have teenagers return their index cards to you. Before you meet with the group again, take some time to write personal responses to your students on their index cards. You may want to keep a notebook or a box containing copies of these index cards.

For more information about the Faith Journal option, refer to page 5 in the Introduction.

Tip From the Trenches

A great way for your teenagers to silently cheer for God is to have them stand and hold their hands over their heads, creating a big "O." If you're in a classroom where you can't make too much noise, have your teenagers stand after each statement and give God a "standing O" (for "ovation").

Tip From the Trenches

To help strengthen the connection between church and home, photocopy the "Taking It Home" page at the end of this study, and either distribute copies to students before they leave or mail them home. Encourage students to complete the reading, activities, and discussion with their families during the coming week.

Music Connection

track 12:
Have students close their eyes and listen to the song "Rejoice." As they listen, have them think of gifts that they are thankful for and ways they can rejoice and praise Jesus for the many gifts they've been given. After the song,

ASK
- **What are some of the gifts you thought of?**
- **How can you rejoice and praise Jesus?**

Have students form trios, and give each trio a sheet of newsprint and markers. Have members of each trio agree on one gift (such as family or health) and write that gift on the top of their newsprint sheet. Then have each trio think of several specific things they would like to do to rejoice and praise God for the gift they've identified.

Rejoice

(recorded by Glisten)

Rejoice—
Lift up your voice and praise
Jesus now.

Rejoice—
Lift up your voice and praise
Jesus now.

Hallelujah!
Hallelujah!
Hallelujah!

Rejoice—
Lift up your voice and praise
Jesus now.

Rejoice—
Lift up your voice and praise
Jesus now.

Hallelujah!
Hallelujah!
Hallelujah!

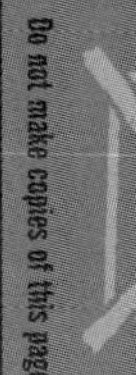

A Strange Event

idea:weird

[t h i n k]

1. Your grandma and grandpa announce at your recent family reunion that God has told them he's going to bless them with a child. They are both ninety years old.

2. One night in church, your grandma announces that she's two months pregnant.

3. While visiting your grandparents one Saturday afternoon, you notice that your grandma's abdomen has gotten quite round. When you ask your grandma about it, she replies, "Oh, dear, that's your new uncle."

4. Your grandfather awakens you at 4:30 in the morning to announce the birth of his and your grandmother's new child. You are astounded.

Talking About It | idea:discuss

Driving Home the Point:

"Let me then not fail to praise my God continually, for it is his due, and it is all I can return for his many favors and great goodness to me; and let me resolve to be virtuous, that I may be happy, that I may please him, who is delighted to see me happy." **(Benjamin Franklin)**

Talking At Home:

Read **Psalm 100** together and answer these questions:

- What gifts has God given us as a family?

- What's the best way to respond as a family to what God has given us?

Have a "joy" party! Share all of the great things God has done for your family!

Desperate Prayers

Genesis 21:8-21

13

God Cares for Hagar and Ishmael

 **key question:** When does God hear us?

 **study focus:** Teenagers will examine how God responds to their prayers when they feel desperate.

key verse: "So I say to you: Ask and it will be given to you; seek and you will find; knock and the door will be opened to you." Luke 11:9

A Look at the Study

Study Sequence	Minutes	What Students Will Do	Classroom Supplies
Getting Started	10 to 15	**Are You Listening, God?**—Discuss their experiences with answered prayers and experience a quote sharing a different view of the way God answers prayers.	Newsprint, marker, tape, "Answered Prayers" handouts (p. 137), pens
Bible Story Exploration	5 to 10	**Hagar and Ishmael's Banishment**—Explore background information about the story of Hagar and Ishmael.	"Historical Context" copies (p. 131), paper, pens
	20 to 25	**Crying Out to God**—Experience the story of Hagar and Ishmael from different characters' points of view, put their own desperate prayers in a "desperate prayer bottle," and discuss faulty analogies people sometimes make for the ways their prayers reach God.	Bible, "Answered Prayers" handouts (p. 137), pens, scrap paper, empty soft drink bottle
Bible Application	5 to 10	**From Your Mouth to God's Heart**—Create their own desperate prayer bottles and then discuss what the Key Verse has to say about God's answers to prayer.	Empty soft drink bottles, corks, decorating supplies, scrap paper, tape, pens, "Answered Prayers" handouts (p. 137)
	up to 5	**Faith Journal**—Explore the Key Question and respond in writing.	Index cards, pens
	up to 5	**Quarter Review**—Reflect on what they've learned.	Newsprint, marker, tape
Music Connection	5 to 10	**Tonight**—Explore how to help someone who is experiencing desperate times. Use this option at an appropriate time in the study.	Bibles, CD: "Tonight" (Track 13), CD player, paper, pens

Age-Level Insight

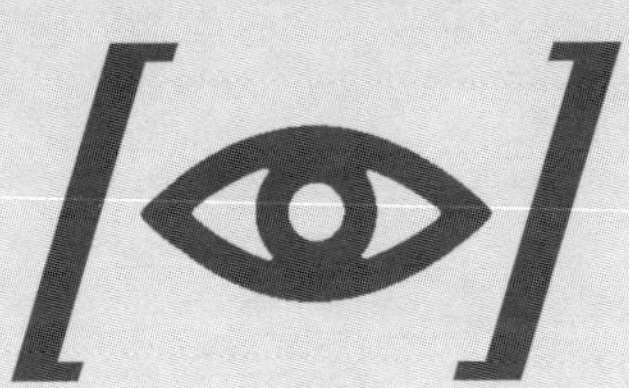

Teenagers can begin to view prayer with an adult understanding. They can view God as a friend they can talk to whenever they want to. They can talk to God about anything and know he cares about the things that make them happy and sad. Teach them about all different aspects of prayer such as praise, intercession, and prayers for forgiveness. Give teenagers opportunities to practice prayer and help them see how it can be a vital part of their lives.

Last Week's Impact

As teenagers arrive, greet them warmly and ask follow-up questions to review last week's study and Key Verse. Ask questions such as "What kinds of gifts has God given your family?" and "How do you respond when God gives you a gift?"

If you used the Faith Journal option last week, take this time to return your students' index cards to them.

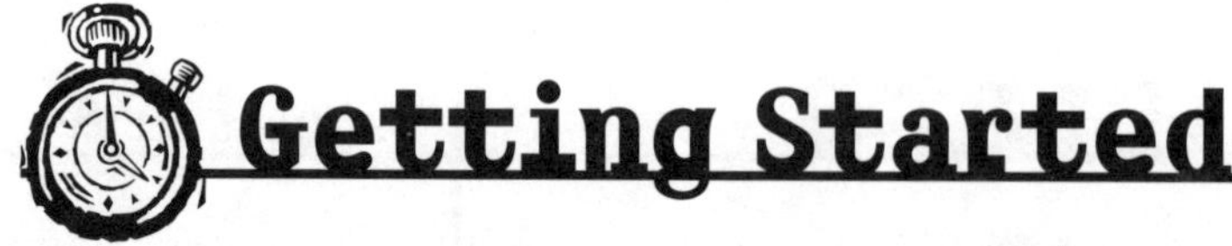

Are You Listening, God?

Write the following statements on newsprint, and tape the newsprint to a wall:

• A time I prayed to God, and God answered my prayer just the way I wanted;

• A time I prayed to God, and God didn't answer my prayer the way I wanted.

Have teenagers form groups of four or fewer, and have group members read the statements on the newsprint and share their experiences involving God's answers to their prayers.

ASK • **Do you believe that God always hears and answers prayers? Why or why not?**

Give each student a copy of the "Answered Prayers" handout (p. 137) and a pen. Have students read the essay within their groups.

ASK • **Do you agree or disagree with the soldier's perspective about answered prayers? Explain.**

Direct groups to follow the directions on the bottom of the handout, helping them to apply the essay to their own lives. When they're finished, have groups share what they came up with.

After the discussion, get everyone's attention.

ASK

• **When does God really hear our prayers?**

• **How can we know we've "gotten through" to God when we pray?**

Read aloud the Key Verse printed at the bottom of the handout.

SAY **In this verse, Jesus proclaimed that God hears us when we pray. But sometimes we don't always get the answers we want, even when we feel desperate. Today we're going to look at someone in Scripture who prayed to God when she felt desperate. We'll compare God's response to her to God's responses in our lives today.**

Encourage students to keep their handouts for later use in the study.

Historical Context | Genesis 21:8-21

It was typical in Abraham's culture to have a celebration when a child was weaned, which was usually around two to three years of age. The celebration for Isaac was probably even bigger than most because he was something of a miracle child.

Unfortunately the joyous occasion soon turned to bitterness. We don't know if Ishmael's mocking of Isaac happened on the day of the celebration, but it must have occurred soon afterward. Ishmael had been born to Abraham through Hagar, Sarah's maidservant, after Sarah decided to take things into her own hands and had Abraham sleep with Hagar to "build a family" (Genesis 16:2). By the time Isaac was two, Ishmael was about sixteen (Genesis 16:16; 21:5).

It's easy to understand why a mother would be upset by a sixteen-year-old teasing her two- or three-year-old. But the animosity ran deeper than the teasing. Sarah and Hagar had been at odds since Hagar was pregnant with Ishmael (Genesis 16:4-10). Abraham's decision to send Hagar and Ishmael away probably had been a long time in coming.

Abraham didn't want to send Hagar and Ishmael away. He knew it was wrong according to his culture and according to anyone's standards of fatherhood. When God told Abraham to go ahead and do what Sarah wanted, God didn't say it was right. But God did promise to take care of Ishmael, eventually making a great nation of his descendants as well as Isaac's.

The area where Abraham lived was desert, so Hagar and Ishmael would have had a tough time finding food and water. The skin of water and the food Abraham gave them was probably as much as they could comfortably carry but wouldn't have lasted very long. Abraham had to have known that without God's help, the two wouldn't live a week.

Remember that Ishmael was at least sixteen by this time. If Hagar had to put him under a bush, he must have been terribly weakened by fluid deprivation. He likely wasn't far from death, as Hagar estimated (Genesis 21:16). We don't know for sure why God responded to Ishmael's crying and not to Hagar's sobs. It may have been because of God's commitment to Abraham to take care of Ishmael.

It seems odd that God responded to Ishmael's cry but sent an angel to speak to Hagar. It may be that Ishmael was simply too weak to even get water for himself. It also seems likely that the well had been there all the time but Hagar didn't see it until God made it visible to her. God was actually there taking care of them and providing the water they needed, but they couldn't see it until they acknowledged their need for God. When they cried out to God, God heard and responded. And we can count on God to always do the same for us!

Bible Story Exploration

Hagar and Ishmael's Banishment

Give each group a copy of the "Historical Context" box (p. 131), paper, and a pen.

SAY **I'd like you to begin your study of the story of Hagar and Ishmael by studying some background information. I'd like each of you to read this information about Hagar and Ishmael. As you're reading, note any important or interesting facts.**

Tip From the Trenches

If students say they have trouble relating to feelings of desperation in Hagar's life, encourage them to consider whether the following descriptions have ever been true of them.

SAY **You have felt desperate if you have ever...**

- **become reckless or violent because of feelings of hopelessness;**
- **tried something extreme, unhealthy, or dangerous as a "last resort" to solve a problem;**
- **suffered from intense feelings of anxiety or unbearable need; or**
- **felt depressed or hopeless about a situation or condition in your life.**

Give students a few minutes to read.

SAY **Now I'd like each group to create a radio script based on the information you just read. You'll need one person in your group to be the announcer. The other people in the group can be either characters or sound effects.**

Give groups a few minutes to create their scripts, and have them present the scripts for the whole group.

ASK • **What does this information tell you about God?**

• **What does the information tell you about humans?**

• **According to your research, when do you think God hears us?**

SAY **Let's learn more about Hagar and Ishmael's relationship with God.**

Crying Out to God

Have students turn over their "Answered Prayers" handouts from the opening activity.

SAY **I'm going to read the story of Hagar and Ishmael aloud. As I read, I'd like you to choose one of the characters in the story you identify with most: Abraham, Hagar, or Ishmael. As you listen, I'd like you to jot down notes about how your character might have been feeling, both physically and emotionally.**

Read **Genesis 21:8-21** aloud slowly.

Have a few volunteers share the feelings of their chosen characters. Then have students form pairs, and have pairs discuss these questions:

- **Which person in this story do you identify with the most? Explain.**
- **If you had been in the desert with Hagar, what would you have told her?**
- **Do you agree with the way God responded to Hagar? Why or why not?**
- **How do you want God to respond to you when you pray?**

Give students each a piece of scrap paper and a pen.

SAY **I'd like you to write a one- or two-sentence description of a time you prayed a desperate prayer to God. For example, you might write about a time when someone you loved died, about your parents divorcing, or about a time you faced a personal problem that seemed overwhelming.**

Give students a minute to write.

SAY **Now on the back of your paper, I'd like you to write a sentence or two about whether God answered your prayers the way you wanted him to.** When students finish, have them share what they wrote with their partners.

Have partners discuss these questions:

- **Based on this experience, do you believe that God always hears us when we pray? Why or why not?**

- **Since God doesn't always respond to our prayers the way we want him to how can we know that God is really hearing us?**

Have students roll up their papers into little scroll shapes, and hold up a large, empty soft drink bottle. Ask students to place their papers inside the bottle, and then close the bottle.

SAY **I'm going to call this our desperate prayer bottle. This bottle represents all the prayers we pray to God during times we feel desperate. The question we have to answer is, "Does God ever hear these prayers?"**

In answer to that question,

SAY **Some people view their desperate prayers as a message in a bottle launched by a person stranded on an island. These people launch their prayers into the "ocean" of the cosmos, hoping that they might someday, somehow, reach God's ears. But they're never really sure that their message gets through to God.**

ASK • **When have you ever felt that way about your desperate prayers? Explain.**

After students share their ideas,

SAY **Other people sometimes view their desperate prayers in the same way a marooned sailor might view a "magic lamp" he finds on the beach. He rubs the lamp three times, believing that whatever he wishes for should be granted.**

ASK • **When have you ever felt that way about your desperate prayers? Explain.**

SAY **Now I'd like you to get back into your groups from the first activity and take a few minutes to come up with your own analogy for ways that people view desperate prayers.**

Give groups a few minutes to do this, and then have them share their analogies with the whole group.

ASK • **Do you think any of these views on prayer is right? Why or why not?**

Teacher Skillbuilder

No matter how great the truth or how important the story, the studies we want students to learn will remain meaningless to them unless we can help them make the truth relevant to their lives. That's why, in this study about Hagar's desperate prayer, students are asked to reveal times they also felt desperate and prayed to God. Even though this exercise may feel awkward at first, encourage students to be honest about their experiences and their desperate feelings. Only by connecting Hagar's experience to their own will they be able to internalize the truth that God hears them when they pray.

For Extra Impact

Have groups find objects in the room to base their analogies on. For example, a group might say, "People view desperate prayers like a mirror. God can see and hear us, but we only see ourselves reflected back."

• When do you think God hears us?

SAY **God heard Hagar when she prayed. God heard her son crying. God hears us when we pray, too—and he does answer us, even if we don't always see his answers right away or understand the answers he gives us.**

Bible Application

From Your Mouth to God's Heart

Give each person an empty soft drink bottle, a cork cut to fit the top of the bottle, and some basic decorating supplies such as tape, colored markers, paper, and scissors.

SAY **Now you're going to make your own desperate prayer bottle. I'd like you to use the materials here to personalize and decorate your bottle, and then create a label with your name on it and tape it to the outside of your bottle.**

When the bottles have been decorated, give each student a piece of scrap paper and a pen.

SAY **Now I'd like you to write a desperate prayer that you have right now on your piece of paper. This could be a prayer about a personal struggle, a prayer about a broken relationship, or even a prayer about the needs of a friend or family member.**

Give students a minute to write.

SAY **As an act of desperate prayer, I'd like you to place your paper inside your desperate prayer bottle and cork it shut.**

When students finish, have them form a circle.

ASK

• Do you believe God always hears and answers our prayers? Why or why not?

SAY **To help you build faith that God will hear and answer your prayers, I'd like you to cut the Key Verse off of the "Answered Prayers" handout and tape the verse to your desperate prayer bottle. I'd like you to think about the verse any time you put a new desperate prayer into your bottle.**

for Younger teenagers

You may want to get younger teenagers started by helping them understand what an analogy is (a comparison of two things based on a similarity between the two).

For Extra Impact

To make the desperate prayer bottle illustration more powerful, go to a local flea market or thrift store before the study and pick up an ornamental, decorative glass bottle to use in your illustration. Create a small label for the bottle that says "Desperate Prayer Bottle."

Tip From the Trenches

If you can't find enough empty soft drink bottles, ask your students the week before to bring in their own, or they can use any jar or bottle available, including peanut butter jars, mayonnaise jars, or baby-food jars. Let students use the jars' lids instead of corks.

As you close, encourage students to keep their desperate prayer bottles and to use them any time they feel desperate and need God's intervention.

Faith Journal

Give students each an index card and a pen. Have teenagers write their names and answers to the following question on their index cards:

- How has God heard and answered some of your personal desperate prayers?

Have teenagers return their index cards to you. Before you meet with the group again, take some time to write personal responses to your students on their index cards. You may want to keep a notebook or a box containing copies of these index cards.

For more information about the Faith Journal option, refer to page 5 in the Introduction.

Quarter Review

Write the following statements on newsprint, and hang the newsprint where students can see it.

- My favorite study this quarter was...
- One thing I learned that I believe has affected me is...
- I plan to share what I've learned with people around me by...

Have students form pairs and take turns finishing the statements in their pairs. When they're finished sharing, have volunteers share their answers with the whole group.

Tip From the Trenches

To help strengthen the connection between church and home, photocopy the "Taking It Home" page at the end of this study, and either distribute copies to students before they leave or mail them home. Encourage students to complete the reading, activities, and discussion with their families during the coming week.

track 13:

Play the song "Tonight." Have students close their eyes and imagine a situation that might lead to the desperate prayer portrayed in the song. After the song, ask:

ASK
- **What were some of the situations that came to mind?**
- **How do you think God might respond to this desperate prayer?**

Have students form pairs, and give each pair a piece of paper and a pen. Have pairs read the Key Verse together. Then have partners work together to write something they might say to someone who was praying the desperate prayer in the song based on the comfort found in the Key Verse.

Tonight

(recorded by Michael Knott)

Jesus, won't you take me in your arms tonight
(tonight, tonight)?
Jesus, won't you save me from harm tonight
(tonight, tonight)?
I didn't know
I didn't know
Which road was wrong,
Which road was right.
Jesus, won't you save me from this blaming voice
tonight (tonight)?
Did I know which road?

[m u s i c]

desperate

Answered Prayers

idea:answers

I asked God for strength, that I might achieve.
I was made weak, that I might learn humbly to obey.
I asked for health, that I might do greater things.
I was given infirmity, that I might do better things.
I asked for riches, that I might be happy.
I was given poverty, that I might be wise.
I asked for power, that I might have the praise of men.
I was given weakness, that I might feel the need of God.
I asked for all things that I might enjoy life,
I was given life that I might enjoy all things.
I got nothing that I asked for—but everything that I had hoped for.
Almost, despite myself, my unspoken prayers were answered.
I am among all men, most richly blessed.

—Anonymous Confederate soldier

In your group, choose two of the five things this soldier was given, and think of some possible examples of these things either from your own life or from the lives of people you know. For example, maybe you know a person who was diagnosed with a life-threatening illness and turned his or her life around.

Key Verse:
"So I say to you: Ask and it will be given to you; seek and you will find; knock and the door will be opened to you" (Luke 11:9).

[t h i n k] everything

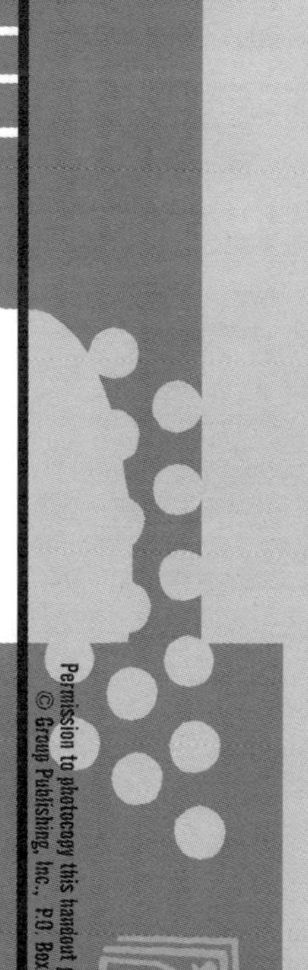

Taking It Home

idea:discuss Talking About It

[take home] with you always

Driving Home the Point:

"When Christa's parents divorced, she wasn't surprised. There had been plenty of clues...But she was surprised by the stormy feelings that welled up within her, especially since she considered herself a 'strong' Christian.

"Christa knew it was normal for Christians to feel crummy at times...But she was afraid to talk to anyone about the depths of her despair... What would [her friends] say if they knew she was just hiding her feelings behind a papier-mache smile that was beginning to crack?

"Then one night as she lay crying in bed, she began to talk to God about the problems she faced...She told God of her feelings of anger, bitterness, and confusion. She told him she felt totally crushed by her parents' situation and that she didn't think she loved her father. She told God there was something inside her that craved a daddy's shoulder to cry on, for a daddy's strong arms to hold her and give her a sense of confidence. Without that, she told God, she didn't feel like a whole person.

"As weeks passed, God became that father she could turn to. That's not to say the going was easy...She was still hurt. But she felt God wanted to help. And by opening her heart to him, she gained a sense of security and confidence to face her problems, and support to work them out."

(S. Rickly Christian, Alive**)**

Talking At Home:

Read **Psalm 23** together and discuss these questions:

• What does this psalm mean to you?

• What does this familiar passage tell us about the ways that God wants to comfort us?

• How can we respond to God's comfort and protection?

When did you feel desperate? What did you do to deal with those feelings? Did you pray to God in desperation? If so, how did God respond?

Evaluation of Group's FaithWeaver™ Bible Curriculum
FaithWeaver Youth Bible Studies: Bible Beginnings

Please help us continue to provide innovative and useful resources for ministry by taking a moment to fill out and send us this evaluation.

• • •

The things I like best about this quarter of curriculum:

This quarter could be improved by:

The things I liked and/or disliked about the CD:

Curriculum I used before using FaithWeaver:

I will use FaithWeaver in future quarters (circle one):

Not Likely				**Definitely**
1	2	3	4	5

How many youth were in your class this quarter?____________________

How many age levels in your church used FaithWeaver this quarter? ____________________

Optional Information:

Name ____

Street Address ____________________________________

City____________________State ____________ ZIP __________

E-mail____

Please mail or fax your completed evaluation to:

Group Publishing, Inc.
Attention: FaithWeaver Feedback
P.O. Box 481
Loveland, CO 80539
Fax: (970) 679-4370

Thank you!

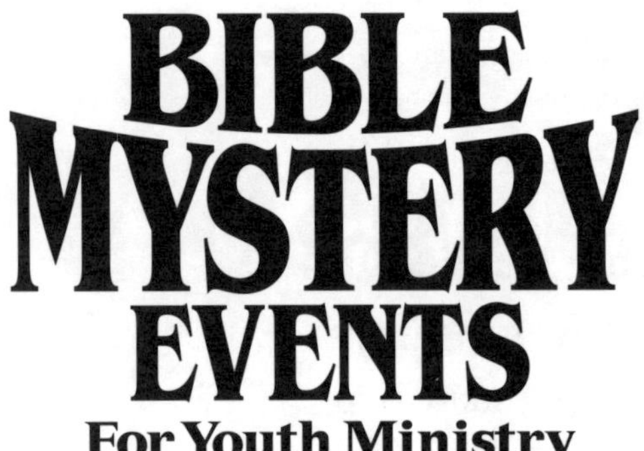

It's a party...a Bible adventure...and a dress-up event—all rolled into one! Teenagers (or adults!) act out roles as they play fun games, and discover new insights into important Bible stories! Each kit comes with everything your group needs to design an event that lasts three hours...or three days...it's up to you! Includes a step-by-step planning guide, Bible-application ideas, event invitations, advertising clip art, and more.

THE CASE OF THE MISSING PROFESSOR

Robert & Linda Klimek

Not much happens in Wallar Hollar...except that the professor has disappeared! Somebody knows more than he or she is saying—but who? This down-home experience raises the same fear...confusion...joy...and surprise experienced by men and women who knew Jesus.

ISBN 1-55945-776-7

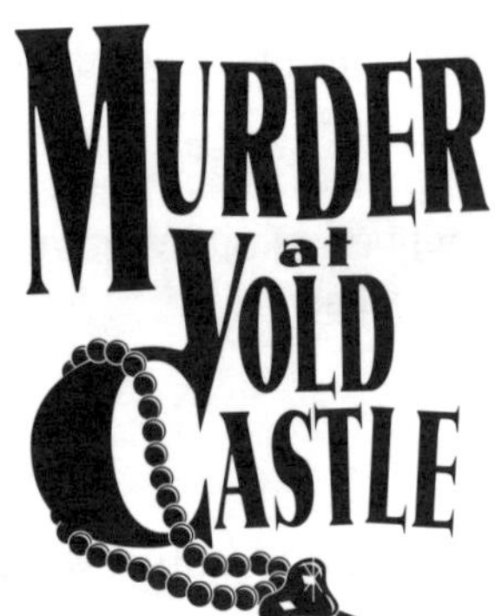

Robert & Linda Klimek

Visitors to this historic fortress discover their host, Baron von Schnell, has been killed...and every guest is a suspect! As your kids act out their roles, they'll experience the same intrigues and conflicts lived out by Saul and David—and prepare for an exciting Bible study.

ISBN 1-55945-694-9

The Great Circus Caper

Robert & Linda Klimek NEW!

Someone is sabotaging this third-generation, family-owned circus, and it's losing money—fast. As group members play the roles of circus acts and a desperate family, they'll discover new insights into the adventures of Moses during the Exodus.

ISBN 0-7644-2116-6

Intrigue on Emerald Pier

Robert & Linda Klimek NEW!

100 years ago, Captain Abel Smith mysteriously drowned in the murky waters near this California town's scenic pier. As group members play the roles of beach characters and shopkeepers, they'll explore four of Jesus' New Testament parables.

ISBN 0-7644-2117-4

Discover our full line of children's, youth, and adult ministry resources at your local Christian bookstore, or write: Group Publishing, P.O. Box 485, Loveland, CO 80539.

EXCITING RESOURCES FOR YOUR CHILDREN'S MINISTRY

NEW!

5-Minute Messages and More

Donald Hinchey

These children's messages are specially designed to give children's workers what they want most: *flexibility*. Simple craft and activity ideas stretch these 29 new messages from 5 minutes up to 12 minutes of meaningful learning...on a moment's notice! So they're ideal for children's church...during church worship services...at a midweek club...or anywhere else multiple ages of children can benefit from hearing God's word!

ISBN 0-7644-2038-0

NEW!

Bold Bible Kids

Encourage children with these 12 character-building lessons, each based on a different child in the Bible. Your kids will discover how God has used little children in *huge* ways—and continues to use kids today! These flexible lessons last between 55 minutes and an hour...the perfect length for most church programs! Plus, they are suitable for multi-age groupings. Includes historical information that helps kids connect with Bible characters, and suggestions for encouraging positive, godly character traits in the lives of your children.

ISBN 0-7644-2114-X

The Children's Worker's Encyclopedia of Bible-Teaching Ideas

New ideas—and lots of them!—for captivating children with stories from the Bible. You get over 340 attention-grabbing, active-learning devotions...art and craft projects...creative prayers...service projects...field trips...music suggestions...quiet reflection activities...skits...and more—winning ideas from each and every book of the Bible! Simple, step-by-step directions and handy indexes make it easy to slide an idea into any meeting—on short notice—with little or no preparation!

Old Testament ISBN 1-55945-622-1
New Testament ISBN 1-55945-625-6

Fun & Easy Games

With these 89 games, your children will *cooperate* instead of compete—so everyone finishes a winner! That means no more hurt feelings...no more children feeling like losers...no more hovering over the finish line to be sure there's no cheating. You get new games to play in gyms...classrooms...outside on the lawn...and as you travel!

ISBN 0-7644-2042-9

EXCITING RESOURCES FOR CHURCH MINISTRY!

The Dirt on Learning NEW!
Thom & Joani Schultz

This thought-provoking book explores what Jesus' Parable of the Sower says about effective teaching *and* learning. Readers will rethink the Christian education methods used in their churches and consider what really works. Use the video training kit to challenge and inspire your entire ministry team and set a practical course of action for Christian education methods that really *work*!

ISBN 0-7644-2088-7 Book Only
ISBN 0-7644-2152-2 Video Training Kit

The Family-Friendly Church
Ben Freudenburg with Rick Lawrence

Discover how certain programming can often short-circuit your church's ability to truly strengthen families—and what you can do about it! You'll get practical ideas and suggestions featuring profiles of real churches. It also includes thought-provoking application worksheets that will help you apply the principles and insights to your own church.

ISBN 0-7644-2048-8

Fun Friend-Making Activities for Adult Groups
Karen Dockrey

More than 50 relational programming ideas help even shy adults talk with others at church! You'll find low-risk Icebreakers to get adults introduced and talking...Camaraderie-Builders that help adults connect and start talking about what's really happening in their lives...and Friend-Makers to cement friendships with authentic sharing and accountability!

ISBN 0-7644-2011-9

Extraordinary Results From Ordinary Teachers
Michael D. Warden

Now both professional *and* volunteer Christian educators can teach as Jesus taught! You'll explore the teaching style and methods of Jesus and get clear and informed ways to deepen your teaching and increase your impact! This is an essential resource for every teacher, youth worker, or pastor.

ISBN 0-7644-2013-5